Illustrated Dogwatching

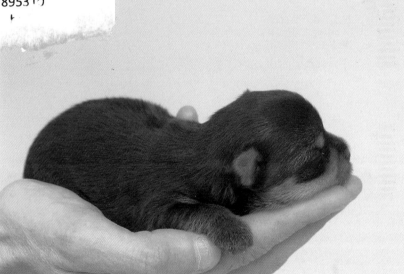

Illustrated
DOGWATCHING

DESMOND
MORRIS

EBURY PRESS
LONDON

First published in 1986 by Jonathan Cape

This edition first published in 1996 by Ebury Press

Paperback edition 1998

1 3 5 7 9 10 8 6 4 2

Designed by David Fordham
Picture research by Nadine Bazar

Ebury Press
Random House, 20 Vauxhall Bridge Road,
London SW1V 2SA

Random House Australia Pty Limited
20 Alfred Street, Milsons Point, Sydney,
New South Wales 2061, Australia

Random House New Zealand Limited
18 Poland Road, Glenfield, Auckland 10, New Zealand

Random House South Africa (Pty) Limited
Endulini, 5 Jubilee Road, Parktown 2193, South Africa

Random House UK Limited Reg. No. 954009

A CIP catalogue record for this book is available from the British Library

ISBN 0 09 186516 6

Printed by Tien Wah Press

CONTENTS

INTRODUCTION

IN THE WHOLE OF HUMAN HISTORY ONLY TWO KINDS OF animals have been allowed the freedom of our homes: the cat and the dog. It is true that in earlier times farm animals were often brought into the home at night for security, but they were always penned or tethered. It is also true that in more recent times a wide variety of pet species have been kept inside our houses – fish in tanks, birds in cages, reptiles in vivaria – but all of these have been captives, separated from us by glass or wire or bars. Only cats and dogs have been permitted to wander from room to room and to come and go almost as they please. With them we have a special relationship, an ancient contract with quite specific terms of agreement.

Sadly, these terms have often been broken, and nearly always by us. It is a sobering thought that cats and dogs are more loyal, trustworthy and reliable than human beings. Very occasionally they turn on us, scratch us or bite us, or run away and leave us, but when this happens there is usually a piece of human stupidity or cruelty lurking in the background to provide a cause. For most of the time they unswervingly fulfil their half of the age-old bargain we have struck with them, and shame us by their conduct.

The contract that was drawn up between man and dog is over 10,000 years old. Had it been written down, it would have stated that if the dog performs certain tasks for us, we in return will provide it with food and water, and with shelter, companionship and care. The tasks it has been asked to carry out have been many and varied. Dogs have been required to guard our homes, protect our persons, aid our hunts, destroy our vermin, and pull our sledges. In more specialized roles, they have been trained to collect birds' eggs in their mouths without breaking the shells, locate truffles, sniff out drugs at airports, guide the blind, rescue avalanche victims, track down escaped criminals, run races, travel in space, act on the stage and in films and compete as show dogs.

Occasionally the faithful dog has been unwittingly reduced to a human level of barbaric conduct. Today we think of the 'dogs of war' as human mercenaries – men who enjoy the macho thrill of maiming and killing with special weapons. But originally they were real dogs, trained to attack the front lines of an enemy army. Shakespeare is referring to this when he makes Mark Antony call out, 'Cry "Havoc!" and let slip the dogs of war'. The ancient Gauls retaliated by sending in armoured dogs, equipped with heavy collars bristling with razor-sharp knives. These terrifying animals, rushing and leaping at the Roman cavalry, tore the legs of their horses to shreds.

Regrettably, fighting dogs are still with us today. Although officially outlawed, pit fights between specially

trained animals remain an excuse for gambling and for the savage entertainment of the more bloodthirsty elements of society. These contests have been forced to go underground but they have by no means been eliminated. In some Eastern countries dogs are considered a food delicacy, but this has never been one of their major roles, and is steadily becoming less common. It appears to have been most widespread in China, where the name of the edible dog was the same as the slang word for food: chow. In most regions, however, dogs escaped the pot because they had so many other, more important uses.

One of the unfortunate side-effects of the great popularity of dogs in all human societies was the growth of the stray dog population. In some countries this canine surplus established itself as a disease-ridden scavenging horde that gave all dogs a bad name. The Pariah Dogs in the Middle East, in particular, turned human friendship into revulsion. In the doctrines of several religions the dog became 'unclean'. Over the years the very word became a term of contempt: dirty dog, filthy cur, pig-dog and dogsbody. Even today, in some ethnic groups, children learn the ancient tradition of despising the dog. The strongest survival of this attitude is found in Muslim cultures. Re-education in schools has proved an uphill struggle.

In the West a happier development has occurred. As the earlier tasks set for the dog have faded in importance, a new role has emerged. The working dog has been largely replaced by the pet dog. True, working dogs still thrive in a number of their old capacities, but they are now greatly outnumbered by the new 'companion dogs'. This is closely linked with the spread of urban and suburban man, and the growth of great cities. In this context there are few tasks for the working dog to perform, but the bond between man and dog is so strong that the complete loss of the canine element in human family life could not be contemplated. As a result, since the Industrial Revolution, many new breeds have been refined. Pedigree standards have been established and dog shows organized. The competitive showing of pedigree breeds has become big business.

At the same time, thousands of mongrel dogs have appeared on the scene. Owners simply wanting a faithful, friendly companion have frequently scorned the highly specialized pedigree breeds, criticizing them as being too artificial, their particular features and qualities taken to worrying extremes, their inbreeding supposedly making them difficult to deal with. The top dog-breeders have denied this and insisted that only with expensive, exclusive dogs is sufficient care taken of the animal's needs. To these breeders, the mongrel-keepers are the thin edge of the wedge that leads to dog neglect, to uncared-for-strays, to

fouling public places and giving dogs a bad name. If all dogs were high-born pedigrees, they argue, anti-dog feelings would vanish and society would value their canine companions as the precious objects which they are.

There is some truth in both viewpoints. Some pedigree breeds have been taken too far, so that the dogs in question now suffer regularly from physical complaints. Dogs with very short legs and very long bodies are prone to slipped discs. Those with flattened faces suffer from breathing difficulties. Others have eye troubles or hip troubles. The people concerned with these suspect breeds tend to keep quiet about the shortcomings that have multiplied over the years, for fear that their particular breed will lose its popularity. This is a pity, as is the trend towards greater and greater exaggeration. Only a hundred years ago, for example, the Bulldog was a comparatively long-legged animal, and the Dachshund had a much shorter body. These are only two of the many breeds where a feature has been magnified little by little until it has caused the 'refined' dogs serious trouble. It would be an easy matter to breed these and other such dogs back — a little way at least — to resemble the kinds of animals they were in earlier centuries, when they were still capable of acting as proper working dogs. They would lose none of their charm and would gain immeasurably in health and fitness.

And the world of the pedigree dog would be the better for it.

The world of the mongrel is more of a problem. It is true that many thousands of mongrel-owners treat their pets with enormous care and respect, but because these animals are of so little commercial value they are also frequently abused. Litters of puppies are sold off cheaply or given away and are then often maltreated or abandoned. Each year London's Battersea Dogs' Home takes in about 20,000 unwanted strays (the figure for 1985 was 19,889, of which 76 per cent were mongrels). And that is just one establishment. Many of these dogs are found new homes, but many more have to be killed. It has been estimated that, in the British Isles alone, 2,000 dogs have to be destroyed every day. It is hard to see how to alter this situation by direct action. The only hope for the future seems to be a general improvement in social attitudes towards animal welfare.

An additional cross which dogs must bear is having to act as the recipients of a great deal of human aggression and scientific curiosity. On both counts, being a dog means suffering pain. Humans are notorious for redirecting their aggression down the social order. The boss insults his aides, they shout at their underlings, the underlings then shout at *their* underlings, and so on, down to the very bot-

tom of the social ladder — where sits the trusting dog. When a dog is kicked and whipped it is hard for it to understand that the rough treatment it is receiving may have begun as a sarcastic phrase in some remote board-room, which then reverberated down the ranks, gaining momentum all the way, until it ended in the dog's yelping agony. Some of the punishments that are meted out to dogs after travelling this route are hard to credit. In Britain alone, the RSPCA receives about 40,000 complaints of cruelty to dogs each year.

Equally hard to believe are some of the cruelties per-formed in the name of scientific research. The excuse for breaking the canine contract in such instances is that the pain inflicted is helping us to advance the sum of human knowledge. We may be betraying the trust dogs put in us, as members of their 'packs', but we can justify this by pub-lishing learned papers of our findings. In reality, the vast majority of all painful experiments carried out on long-suf-fering dogs fail to advance human knowledge in any appre-ciable way. In the early days of physiology, medicine, and zoology, there may have been some value in the lessons that were learnt, but today this is rarely the case. The dog should be left in peace, but this is unlikely to happen.

This brings me to the primary purpose of writing *Dogwatching*, which is to demonstrate that by simple, direct

observation, or by observational experiments which cause the dogs involved no harm, it is possible to understand and appreciate these remarkable animals in great and surprising detail. They have so much to offer us. They are playful companions when we are in the mood for fun; they are loving companions when we are lonely or depressed; they are health-giving companions when they stir us into taking long walks; they are calming companions when we become agitated, apprehensive or tense; and they still carry out their age-old duties of alerting us to intruders in our homes and protecting us from attack — to mention only two of their surviving work-roles.

Those disturbed individuals who pour out hatred for dogs are missing a great deal. And those who are merely disinterested are also losing out on an amazingly rewarding man/animal relationship. Since such people will almost cer-tainly ignore this book, they will be unaware of an intrigu-ing fact: people who keep dogs (or cats, for that matter) live longer on average than those who do not. This is not some kind of pro-canine campaigning fantasy. It is a simple medical fact that the calming influence of the company of a friendly pet animal reduces blood pressure and therefore the risk of heart attack. To stroke a cat, pat a dog or cud-dle any sort of furry pet has a de-stressing influence that goes directly to the root of many of today's cultural

ailments. Most of us suffer from too much tension and stress in the hustle of modern urban living, where minute-by-minute considerations are frequently complex and demand a whole range of conflicting compromises. By contrast, the friendly contact of a pet dog or cat serves to remind us of the survival of simple, direct innocence even inside the dizzy whirlpool we refer to as civilization.

Unfortunately, even those who benefit from this animal relationship frequently fail to realize what a fascinating animal the dog really is. It is so familiar to us all that we start to take it for granted. If we do ask questions about the dog: how sensitive is its nose? can it see colours? how does it find its way home when lost? why does it wag its tail when greeting us? why does it have such a strange sex life? ... and so on, we often shrug and then move on to something else, without ever bothering to find out the answers. The routine dog books tend to skip over the most basic questions and concentrate instead on such subjects as dog-grooming, feeding, veterinary care and the distinguishing characteristics of the several hundred breeds that now exist. This is all useful information, but we still want to know why some dogs howl more than others, and why they all bark so much, and why dogs behave in the way that they do. I have therefore set out to answer such key questions in a series of short, simple answers. By laying out the text in this manner I hope that you will be able to use the book to deal with each question that comes up in your human/dog relationship, and also that, by browsing through it, you will increase your appreciation of the extraordinary end-product of canine evolution that leaps up to greet you every time you return home and open your front door.

THE DOG

WHY IS THE DOG SO SPECIAL? WHAT IS IT ABOUT THE canine personality that has singled this animal out from all the 4,236 species of non-human mammals to be man's closest companion? The answer is one that some people may find disturbing, for 'man's best friend' is, in reality, a wolf in dog's clothing. And it is the wolf's personality that is the key to understanding our strong bond with the dog.

The idea that all our dogs, from scruffy mongrels to haughty show champions, from mangy strays to perfect pedigrees, and from tiny Chihuahuas to gigantic Great Danes, are nothing more or less than domesticated wolves is, for some, a little hard to swallow. The thought upsets them because of the long tradition of horror stories connected with the wild wolf. There is the savage wolf and the man-eating wolf, the werewolf and the big bad wolf. Scarcely a kind word anywhere for this magnificent creature until we come to the modern, objective studies of the last few decades. So it is hard to blame people for rejecting out of hand the suggestion that the cheerful, harmless little pooch sitting on the rug, looking up at them with big friendly eyes, is really a member of the same species as the mighty wolf. But this is something we have to accept, not just because it is true, but because it is the only way to comprehend the behaviour of the domestic dog and to

appreciate why it is that dogs rather than, say, monkeys, bears or racoons, have become man's best friend.

Before considering the behaviour of the wolf, we can dispose of some obvious objections to this idea. Domestic dogs vary enormously in shape, size and colour, so surely they cannot all belong to the same species? Yes, they can and they do. The variations may be dramatic but they are rather superficial. Any breed of dog can interbreed with any other and produce fertile offspring. The genetic differences that have been cultivated by pedigree breeding are far too small to have isolated one breed from another at the biological level. But supposing a male Chihuahua becomes aroused by the heady fragrance of a Great Dane bitch on heat? What can he do about it? He is not a mountaineer. True, but if the bitch in question were artificially inseminated with a sperm sample collected from him, she would become pregnant and produce a litter. As far as we know at present, no two dog breeds are genetically incompatible. Nor, incidentally, is there any difficulty in crossing domestic dogs with wild wolves. They too produce fertile offspring.

So despite appearances to the contrary, all dogs are biologically the same species. The 300-pound St Bernard may be 300 times the weight of the little miniature Yorkshire Terrier, and the Great Dane standing forty

inches at the shoulder may be over ten times its height, but all are brothers beneath the skin. Anyone who has owned a very small dog will confirm this. They may be tiny in size, but inside they know perfectly well that they are mighty wolves and act accordingly. They will give the postman the loud bark or the deep-throated growl they consider he deserves for approaching their personal territory. If the sound comes out as a thin, yapping sound, that is not their fault. And if they happen to meet a big dog in a park, they give it the same treatment. They know that they themselves are fully mature adults, so why should they hold back? The big dogs are sometimes nonplussed by this behaviour, and may even make a dignified retreat in the face of a combined assault from a group of diminutive snappers. If the owners of the big dogs are unhappy about this apparent show of cowardice, they are misinterpreting their pets' behaviour. The big dogs are not afraid of the little ones. Their problem is that the small size of their assailants put the little dogs into a special social category, that of 'puppy'. And there are strong inhibitions about attacking puppies. The problem is that *these* puppies are not behaving like puppies, hence the perplexed response of the larger dogs.

If the six million dogs in Britain, the forty million dogs in the United States, and all the other many millions around the globe, belong to one and the same species, how is it that they have come to look so different from one another? The answer is that the dog, being man's oldest domestic animal, has had plenty of time to become specialized by controlled breeding. Difficult, over-nervous and over-aggressive individuals have been largely eliminated. Dogs have become more juvenile and playful, more placid and amenable. If they have been bred for high-speed chasing, their legs have become longer and their bodies more slender; if they have been bred for 'going to earth' after vermin, their legs have become shorter; if they have been bred as lap dogs, their bodies have been shrunk down and down until they are small enough to pick up and carry with ease. Each of these changes has been made by selective breeding. Miniaturizing a breed, for instance, is straightforward. All you have to do is pick the runts from each litter and breed from these over and over again. In a few generations it is possible to produce dogs of a much reduced stature.

Several hundred 'pure' breeds have been established in recent years in connection with competitive dog shows, and fixed standards laid down for each one. Six main groups of breeds are officially recognized: the gun-dogs, the hounds, the working dogs, the terriers, the toy dogs and the utility dogs.

The gun-dogs are the Pointers, Setters and Retrievers which accompany the hunters and aid them in detecting, driving and recovering game. The hounds help to track down and catch prey that is pursued on horse or on foot. Foxhounds move fast and are suitable for horse accompaniment. Basset-hounds had their legs shortened by selective breeding to slow them down for hunters on foot. Some hounds, such as the Bloodhound, work by scent, others, such as the Greyhound, by sight.

The working dogs include guard-dogs and sheepdogs and certain other breeds with specific functions, such as the sledge-pulling Huskies. The terriers are the small vermin-killers, generally with legs short enough for them to go to earth in pursuit of badgers, foxes and rodents. They have an unusually stubborn and independent personality, originally linked to the need for them to keep after their prey when isolated and working alone.

The toy dogs are essentially dwarf breeds reduced in size to create more manageable pets. Some, such as the Maltese and the Pekinese, have an ancient history as high-status favourites of the rich and powerful, bred for many centuries in their specialized role and with no other, more mundane, working duties in their aristocratic background. The utility group cannot make this élitist boast. They are dogs which, although today acting exclusively as pets and

show dogs, were not so long ago working dogs of one kind or another. They include such varied breeds as the Dalmatian – bred as a flashy coach-dog to run alongside its master's coach-and-horses, the Bulldog – developed as a savage attacker in early bull-baiting contests, and the Lhasa Apso – whose original duty was to sound the alarm if intruders attempted to enter the Dalai Lama's great palace at Lhasa in Tibet. All these tasks have now faded into history but the breeds have survived, hence the rather unromantic name of 'utility dogs'.

In addition to all these aristocrats of the dog world there are the many mongrels and feral dogs. One authority has estimated that there is a world population of 150 million of such animals alive today. Some returned to a wild existence many centuries ago. The Dingo of Australia and the New Guinea Singing Dog are two examples of this type. Others have gone wild or been abandoned in recent years and have established themselves as packs of feral dogs, usually surviving by scavenging on the left-overs of human society. Both these categories have managed to re-adapt to wild conditions despite the fact that they are domesticated animals. They breed among themselves, creating a viable population of independent dogs. A third category is the stray, an abandoned dog which is barely surviving and which has not managed to re-establish itself

as an active member of canine society. Finally, there are the much-loved pet mongrels, kept and cared for by owners who stoutly defend them against the 'pampered pedigrees'. Mongrels, they argue, are much closer to the ancestral dog, which is why they live longer than pedigree dogs, suffer from far fewer physical defects, are more resistant to disease and have a more stable personality, showing far less nervousness and aggression. The hybrid vigour of the mongrel, they claim, makes it the tough, resilient dog it is. Their defence of the mongrel is admirable but unfair, in fact, to the majority of pedigree dogs. The truth is that all modern dogs remain remarkably close to the ancestral type. Whatever their shape, colour or size, they are all basically wolves beneath the skin and we are fortunate that this is so, as will become clear in a moment.

There have been three theories concerning the origin of the domestic dog. One idea envisages a 'missing link' – an ancient wild species of dog, looking rather like the modern Dingo, that gave rise to the domestic dog and was then itself exterminated by early man. In terms of animal husbandry this makes sense, because once a species has been 'improved' by domestic breeding, the human populations concerned have usually taken steps to eliminate the 'unimproved' wild relatives of their animals, to prevent contamination. Also, it is clear that when tame dogs go wild and

start to breed in feral packs, they revert to a similar type all over the world. The Dingoes of Australia, the Singing Dogs of New Guinea, the Pye-Dogs of Asia, the Pariah Dogs of the Middle East and the Indian Dogs of the Americas all look remarkably similar in build and general shape. It is as if they are trying to tell us what their ancient and now extinct ancestor looked like. Despite this, the missing link theory is no longer widely accepted.

A second theory sees different breeds of dog stemming from two wild dog species. Some are thought to be descended from the wolf and some from the jackal. This view was popularized by Konrad Lorenz in his book *Man Meets Dog*, but later research showed this 'double origin' theory to be unfounded. Careful studies of jackals revealed that they are in fact very different both from dogs and from wolves. At the same time, investigation of wolves showed that they are amazingly similar to dogs in almost all respects.

It is the third theory that is now generally accepted, namely, that all modern domestic dogs have descended, during a period of between 8,000 and 12,000 years, from one species alone: the wolf. Meticulous anatomical and behavioural studies have confirmed this during the past few decades and the conclusion now seems inescapable. The one obvious question, however, is why do feral dogs

not revert to a more wolflike type? This question is based on a misunderstanding about the kind of wolf involved in the development of the dog. Today, in films and in zoos, the wolves we see are typically those from the frozen north – the Russian, Scandinavian and Canadian Timber Wolves. They are huge, thick-coated beasts adapted to the coldest area of the original wolf range. The dog is not likely to have developed from these but from the smaller, less stocky, less heavily furred Asiatic Wolf that was common in warmer parts of the range of the species. This animal was much closer in build and appearance to the feral dogs of today and makes the perfect ancestor.

Field-observations of packs of wild wolves have told us a great deal about the true nature of this 'marauding monster'. Far from being a savage beast, it is a species with an impressive social organization, involving a great deal of restraint, rank order control and mutual aid within the pack. Healthy competition between individuals is balanced by active co-operation of several kinds – on the hunt, during defence and when breeding. Adults other than parents will assist in the feeding of the young and there is very little fighting within each social group.

It is clear that it was the great similarity between the social life of wolves and that of early men that led to the tight bond of attachment that grew up between them.

Both of these species lived in 'packs', in a defended group territory. Both of them established a home base in the centre of the territory, from which they made sorties in search of food. Both of them became co-operative hunters specializing in prey bigger than themselves. Both of them employed cunning on the hunt, using encircling tactics and ambushes. Both developed male/female attachments and care of the young by the group. Both evolved a complex set of body signals, including facial expressions, postures and gestural movements.

In the very first instance, the contact between prehistoric men and wolves must have been as competitors, since their ways of life were so similar. Helpless young wolf-cubs were probably taken back to human settlements as juicy morsels for a leisurely meal, but were then allowed to roam around as playthings for human toddlers in the camp. Because there is a special phase in wolf-cub growth when the young animals become 'socialized', those taken young enough would grow up to think of themselves as belonging to a human pack rather than a lupine one. This would have meant that, as they became adult, they would have acted automatically as guard-dogs, raising the alarm if their sharp ears picked up any sound of someone approaching the camp at night. Also, they might have tagged along on the hunts, scenting the prey before their

adopted human companions could detect it. It would have required a very stupid human not to have spotted the value of these canine talents and to realize their potential. Instead of eating all the captive cubs, they would have allowed some to live, remain in the camp and even breed there. Any individuals that were too aggressive or timid would quickly be despatched and eaten. The rest would become partners – symbionts – in the human scheme of things.

As the centuries sped past, the original wolf-type dog probably changed comparatively little, although there may have been some superficial alterations in appearance. Any strange colour forms that cropped up, such as black, white, spotted or blotched, would have been favoured as ways of identifying individual animals, but beyond that there was probably little pressure to modify the prehistoric canine companion.

Eventually, with the advent of farming, the protection of property grew more important and guard-dogs probably then became a specialized breed, as did the hunting dogs and those employed for herding.

But the hundreds of different breeds we know today would still be far, far off in the future. They are a result of greatly speeded-up breeding programmes of a highly selective kind during the past few hundred years. In the Middle

Ages there were probably no more than about a dozen different types of dog in Europe, each one with a major task to perform.

The great explosion of different dog breeds owes its ignition to the Industrial Revolution which made so many dogs, either directly or indirectly, surplus to requirements. Unable to employ them for tasks that were no longer available, and forbidden to use them for cruel sports such as bull-baiting, badger-baiting and dog-fighting, dog enthusiasts had to find some new role for their animals. Competitions for 'best dogs' were arranged in pubs in the eighteenth century and, by the nineteenth, there were fully organized dog shows with fixed standards. Even the Royal Family participated, and pedigree dog-breeding, keeping and showing were soon all the rage.

As the cities rapidly grew during the course of the nineteenth century, the sudden blossoming of pet dogs and companion dogs provided the urbanites with a nostalgic reminder of country life. Walking the dog in the park became almost the last remnant of rural pleasures left for those trapped in the city whirl. In an environment paved with stone and walled with bricks and mortar, the need for some sort of contact with the natural world was a powerful one, and dogs went a long way to fulfilling this need. As they do to this day.

WHY DO DOGS BARK?

IT IS A COMMON ERROR TO IMAGINE THAT A BARKING dog is threatening you. It may be making a loud noise which appears to be aimed directly at you, but this is misleading. For the bark is a canine alarm call and is meant for other members of the pack, including the human pack to which the dog belongs.

The message of the bark is 'there is something strange happening over here. Be alert!' In the wild it has two effects: it causes puppies to take cover and hide, and it arouses adults to assemble for action. In human terms it is rather like the sounding of a bell, beating of a gong, or blowing of a horn to announce that 'someone is approaching the gates' of a fortress. The alarm does not yet tell us whether the arrivals are friends or foes, but it ensures that necessary precautions can be taken. This is why loud barking may greet the arrival of a domestic dog's master, as well as the intrusion of a burglar. Once the new arrival has been identified, the barking is then replaced either by a friendly greeting ceremony or by a serious attack.

Out-and-out attack is, by contrast, completely silent. The fearlessly aggressive dog simply rushes straight at you and bites. Demonstrations of police dogs attacking men pretending to be fleeing criminals confirm this. As the man with the heavily padded arm runs away across the field and the police dog is released by its handler, there is no bark-ing, no sound at all. The silent bounding of the big dog quickly ends with it clamping its jaws on to the padded arm and clinging on tightly.

Fleeing is equally silent. The dog trying desperately to escape keeps quiet as it scampers off into the distance. Vocalizations are essentially indications of conflict or frustration. The fact that they nearly always accompany aggressive encounters with dogs means simply that even the most hostile of canines is usually also slightly afraid. The complete silence of the all-out attack of the police dog is less common than the snarling attack. Snarling, with the lips retracted to display the canine teeth, is typical of the dog which is strongly aggressive and only mildly fearful. The slight tinge of fear is what converts the silent attack into the snarling one, but this is not a dog to be trifled with. The urge to attack is still much too strong in relation to the urge to escape. A snarling dog is a postman's nightmare.

Next, in order of increasing fear, is the growling dog. Growling is slightly more fearful than snarling, but the risk of attack remains great. The growler may feel more on the defensive, but there remains a high level of aggression, sufficient to explode into a full attack at any moment.

When the balance tips a little further away from pure attack and fear begins to gain the upper hand, the growling begins to alternate with barking. The low growl 'expands'

suddenly into a loud bark. This is repeated: growl-bark, growl-bark. The message from such a dog is 'I would like to attack you (growl-) but I think I will call up reinforcements (-bark).'

If the fear element grows stronger and begins to dominate the aggression, inside the brain of the dog, then the growling element in the display disappears and barking alone is heard, loudly and repeatedly. It may continue for an irritatingly long time, until either the strange element causing it has vanished, or the human 'pack' has come to investigate what is going on.

The unique characteristic of domestic dog-barking is that it is delivered in machine-gun bursts: rau-rau-rau ... rau-rau-rau-rau-rau-rau ... rau ... rau-rau-rau, and so on, in an excited stream of powerful noise. This is something for which we have to thank 10,000 years of selective dog-breeding, rather than attributing it to the wild ancestry of our domestic animals. Wolves bark, but the noise they make when they do so is far less impressive. The first time you hear barking in a wolf-pack, you recognize it immediately for what it is, but find it hard to believe that it can be so modest and so abbreviated. Wolf-barking is not particularly loud, or particularly common, and is always monosyllabic. It is best described as a staccato 'wuff' sound. It is usually repeated a number of times, but it never develops

into the noisy machine-gun fire so typical of the wolf's domestic descendants.

Curiously enough, it has been reported that wolves kept near to domestic dogs actually learn to give the amplified dog-bark after a while. So, clearly the transition from wuff to superbark is not too difficult. Despite this learning ability, it is highly likely that, back in the early centuries of the dog's domestication, there was a fairly rapid selection by ancient dog-owners for an improved 'barker' to act as a canine burglar alarm. Building on the modest wolf-wuff, they selected the loudest and most persistently vocal pups from their litters, until the present, noisy guard-dogs were developed. Today almost all dog breeds contain the genetic qualities which give them an improved bark, some breeds being more impressive than others in this respect. Only the Basenji, or African Barkless Dog, seems to have escaped this trend completely. This particular breed was developed as a small, silent hunting dog in ancient Egypt over 5,000 years ago and in its long domestic history has apparently never been put on guard duty.

To sum up, it can be said that the well-known saying that 'his bark is worse than his bite' is based on a canine truth. For the dog that barks is not usually brave enough to bite, and the dog that bites does not bother to bark up reinforcements with the canine alarm call.

WHY DO DOGS HOWL?

ALTHOUGH DOGS BARK MORE THAN WOLVES, THEY howl less. The reason for the comparative rarity of dog-howling is the difference in the social life of the domestic dog and the wild wolf. The function of the howl is to synchronize and assemble the pack for action. Wolves howl most in the early evening before departing on a group hunt and in the early morning before setting off once again. Domestic dogs, with their food presented to them by their owners, live a life of perpetual puppydom, and the need to 'reinforce pack cohesion' (to give howling its official function) is not one of their priorities. The pack-scattering that provokes howling rarely occurs among them. The only time that something like it intrudes on the daily routine of the domestic dog is when an animal is forcibly shut away on its own. It may then perform the 'howl of loneliness' which has the same function as group howling. Both say: 'I (we) are here ... where are you? ... come and join me (us).' In the wild, the effect of this howling is to attract the other members of the pack like a magnet, and to induce them to join in the 'song of the tribe'. Humans who fail to respond to a howling dog by not 'joining it' are derelict in their canine duty.

Some male dogs that never howl under normal circumstances are known to do so with prolonged and heartbreakingly forlorn tones when they are firmly shut away from an attractive bitch on heat. This does not mean that howling is a sexual signal, merely that this is yet another social context in which the basic message is 'join me'.

So powerful is this message of howling that human field-workers have been able to employ fake howling to catch young wolf-cubs. Sitting in a tree and imitating the howling of adult wolves is sometimes sufficient to bring the small cubs tottering out to join the howlers. Older wolves refuse to be fooled by this strategy, however, which reveals an important extra element in the message of the call. As they mature, each wolf comes to recognize the individual identity of the howler.

Even the human field-workers themselves can identify the different members of the pack they are studying in this way. There are slight variations in the singsong sequence of the howling which become personal signature tunes. So the message is 'It is me, come and join me.' The full message may give even more detail. Wolf experts believe that each howling also transmits information about the precise mood of the howlers, as they throw back their heads and give mournful voice. And because howling is more common at the borders of a pack's territory, it would seem that there is also an element of territorial display involved, letting other groups know that a particular zone is occupied by an organized band.

It is significant that solitary wolves – ones that have been driven out of the pack – do not join in the group howlings from their distant corners. Nor do they try to rejoin their original pack. But they do howl on their own from time to time, when the rest of the pack is quiet. If they are answered by other wolf outcasts, this enables them to join up and start a new pack in some other, unoccupied territory.

Returning to the domestic dog, it is clear why they are less prone to howling than their wild cousins. The appropriate social contexts are not there to provoke it. If pet dogs were kept in large groups that had the semblance of pack organization, howling would undoubtedly recur, as it does in some professional kennels. Also, if dogs are shut in

alone, or kept from bitches on heat, or if they are thrown out to become lonely stray dogs, they may howl. But the adult domestic dog that lives in the heart of a caring human family is simply not stimulated to produce this most haunting of all canine cries.

There is one amusing exception to this last statement and that concerns musical families. In pre-television days, when families indulged in evening singsongs, certain pet dogs mistook the signals and assumed that their owners were trying to 'draw the pack together for concerted effort'. Enthusiastically answering the call to hunt by throwing back their heads and howling along with the rest of their adopted pack, they must have been nonplussed by the generally negative reactions this produced.

III

WHY WAS IT BELIEVED THAT IF A DOG HOWLED SOMEONE WOULD DIE?

FROM ANCIENT TIMES THERE HAS BEEN A SUPERSTITIOUS belief that unusual cries from a dog are a warning of impending death and disaster. The dog was supposed to have supernatural powers enabling it to foresee the future, especially when some calamity was approaching. Despite this, the dog was not blamed for the events which followed, or looked upon as an evil creature because of its association with death. Instead it was thought of as 'man's best friend' trying desperately to warn its owners of imminent danger.

Rejecting the supernatural explanation, one authority has put forward the theory that the dogs in question had rabies. When a dog suffers from this disease, it howls and whines and makes strange noises that people cannot fail to notice. If the dog infected its owner, who then died, people hearing of the story were told that the owner met with disaster not long after the dog was heard making unusual sounds. In the era before the transmission of infection was understood, it is easy to see how this link between dog-cries and human death could be interpreted as an omen.

IV

WHY DOES A DOG WAG ITS TAIL?

I T IS OFTEN SAID, BY LAYMEN AND EXPERTS ALIKE, THAT IF a dog wags its tail it must be friendly. This is not so. The error is similar to the one made by people who insist that if a cat wags its tail it must be angry. The only emotional condition which all tail-waggers (both canine and feline) share is a state of conflict. This is true of almost all back-and-forth movements in animal communications.

When an animal is in conflict it feels pulled in two different directions at the same time. It wants to advance and retreat simultaneously, or to turn left and turn right. Since each urge cancels the other out, the animal stays where it is, but in a state of tension. The body, or part of it, begins to move off in one direction, obeying one urge, then stops and moves in the opposite direction. This leads to a whole range of stylized visual signals in the body language of the different species. There are neck-twistings, head-bobbings, leg-bendings, foot-jiggings, shoulder-turnings, body-leanings, tail-flickings and – in cats and dogs – the well-known tail-waggings.

What exactly is happening in the mind of the tail-wagging dog? Essentially the animal wants to stay and wants to go away. The urge to go away is simple – it is caused by fear. The urge to stay is more complex. In fact, there is not one urge but several. The dog may wish to stay because it is hungry, friendly, aggressive, or for any other reason. This

is why it is impossible to label tail-wagging as having a single meaning. It is a visual signal that must always be read in context, along with the other actions that are taking place at the same time. Some examples will help to clarify this:

Puppies do not wag their tails when they are very young. The earliest recorded tail-wag was observed in a seventeen-day-old pup, but this was unusual. By thirty days about 50 per cent of pups are tail-wagging and the activity reaches full maturity at the age of forty-nine days. (These are average figures, there being some breed variation.) The context in which wagging first appears is when the puppies are feeding from the bitch. As they line up along her belly and she starts to suckle them, their tails begin to wag furiously. It is easy to interpret this as 'friendly delight' on the part of the young animals, but if this were so, then why did the wagging not show itself earlier, when the puppies were, say, two weeks old? The milk was just as important to them then and their tails were well enough developed, so what was missing? The answer is inter-puppy conflict. At the age of two weeks the pups cuddle up together for warmth and comfort, but there is as yet no serious rivalry. By the age of six or seven weeks, however, when the tail-wagging is reaching its full expression, the pups have arrived at the social stage of bullying and rough-and-tumble. To feed from the mother they must come very close together –

together – close to the same bodies that were just now nipping and chasing them. This causes fear, but the fear is overpowered by the urge to feed from the closely spaced teats. So when they are being suckled, the pups are in a state of conflict between hunger and fear – wanting to stay at the teat and not wanting to be too close to the other pups. It is this conflict that gives rise to the earliest expression of tail-wagging in dogs.

The next context in which it appears is when the pups are food-begging from the adult animals. The same conflict is in operation here. As the young come close to the mouth of the adult, to seek food there, they are again forced into close proximity with one another.

Later, as adults, when they greet one another after a separation, they add tail-wagging to their other re-contact signals. Here, friendliness and apprehension combine to produce the emotional conflict. Wagging also accompanies sexual advances, where sexual attraction and fear are simultaneously present. And, most important, it is seen when some aggressive approaches are made. In these instances the tail-wagging animal, although hostile, is also fearful – once again a conflict of simultaneous moods.

The quality of the wagging varies. In more submissive animals, the wags are loose and wide. In aggressive animals they are stiff and short. The more subordinate a tail-wagger is, the lower it holds the wagging tail. The confident animal wags a tail that is fully erect.

If all this can be observed by watching dogs (or wolves) encountering one another in a variety of social contexts, why has tail-wagging so often been misunderstood and labelled simply a sign of friendliness? The answer is that we are much more familiar with man/dog greetings than we are with dog/dog greetings. If we have several dogs, they are usually together all the time, but we and they are repeatedly parting and reuniting every day. So what we see, time and again, is the friendly, submissive dog greeting its master or mistress, on whom it looks as the dominant member of its 'pack'. Its overpowering mood on these occasions is one of friendliness and excitement at seeing its pack leader again, but this attraction is tinged with slight apprehension, which is enough to trigger the conflict-response of tail-wagging.

We find this hard to accept because we do not like to think that our dogs have anything but love for us. The idea that they also fear us slightly does not appeal to us. But think of our size in relation to theirs. We tower over them and this alone is worrying for them. Add to this the fact that we are dominant over them in so many ways and they are dependent on us for so many aspects of their survival, and it is not really surprising that their mood is a mixed one.

Finally, in addition to their visual signals, tail-wags are also believed to transmit odour signals. Again, this is not at all easy for us to understand unless we make ourselves contemplate the world from the viewpoint of the dog. Dogs have personal scents that are transmitted from anal glands. Tense, vigorous tail-wagging movements have the effect of rhythmically squeezing these glands. If the tail is in an upright position, as it is with confident dogs, the rapid and rhythmic flagging of the tail will dramatically increase the ejection of anal scents from these glands. Although our human noses are not efficient enough to appreciate these personal scents, they have very great significance for the animals themselves. It is this added bonus that has undoubtedly led to the major role that the simple to-and-fro conflict movement of tail-wagging now enjoys in canine social life.

V

WHY DO DOGS PANT SO MUCH?

PEOPLE PANT AFTER RUNNING TO CATCH A BUS, BUT no human being pants quite so much as a dog. A dog may start panting without even moving its body. If it begins to overheat it simply opens its mouth wide, lets its tongue flop out and begins the rapid, heavy panting with which we are all familiar. While it is doing this, it repeatedly moistens its huge tongue to step up the evaporation process which is the key to the cooling mechanism. Overheated dogs will drink more than usual to maintain the supply of liquid to the tongue's surface. Without this facility, many a dog would have died from heatstroke.

Why do dogs require such a powerful panting mechanism to aid them in regulating their body temperature? The answer lies in the anatomy of their skin. Unlike us, they only possess efficient sweat glands on their feet. We can lose heat rapidly by extensive body sweating, but they cannot.

Curiously, our three closest animal companions, the horse, the cat and the dog, have each evolved a different method of keeping cool. Horses sweat copiously, as we do. Cats lick their fur vigorously when they are too hot, spreading saliva over themselves as a cooling agent. And dogs pant.

The choice of panting by canines undoubtedly has to do with the very heavy coats worn by their ancient ancestors.

It was apparently more important to keep warm in cold weather than cool in hot weather, at the time when the primeval dog was evolving. With a thick coat of fur, there was little that the skin sweat glands could do to help with temperature regulation, and they ceased to be important. Today, with many breeds having thinner coats, sweating could once again come to their owners' assistance on hot afternoons, but the necessary re-evolution of efficient sweat glands has not accompanied the genetic changes in coat type.

Even the naked-skinned breeds of dog, such as the Mexican Hairless Dog, for which sweating could easily become functional again, have remarkably dry skins, even under hot conditions. The body temperature of these strange dogs was once claimed to be as high as 104°F (instead of the usual canine temperature of 101-102°F), but recent tests could not confirm this. They appear to have just the same temperature as other dogs, but their skin *feels* much hotter because it is naked to the touch.

It is said that this breed was developed by the early Mexicans to function as a living hot-water bottle on cold nights, and the absence of canine skin-sweating, combined with a normal temperature that is higher than that of humans, would certainly make it ideal in this role.

VI

WHY DO DOGS COCK THEIR LEGS?

EVERYONE IS BY NOW FAMILIAR WITH THE FACT THAT, for male dogs, urination is much more than the mere elimination of waste substances from the body. Every time they are taken for a walk, the main focus of interest is in reading the chemical signals deposited on scent-posts of various kinds in their home range by the leg-cocking urinations of other male dogs. Every tree-stump and lamp-post is sniffed with quivering concentration. Then, after its odour messages have been carefully read, the dog leaves its own scent-mark, obliterating the older deposit with its own powerful odour.

When they are puppies, both males and females squat to urinate, but at puberty, around the age of eight or nine months, male dogs begin to lift one back leg when squirting their jet of urine. The raised leg is stretched out stiffly, with the body of the dog angled so that the stream of liquid is aimed sideways, instead of downwards onto the ground below. So powerful is the urge to perform this leg-cocking that, on a long scent-filled walk, a dog may run out of urine and find itself unable to produce a jet of liquid. Male dogs can be observed desperately trying to squeeze out a few more drops in order to leave their 'calling card'. Even when the bladder is completely empty they will continue to perform the leg-raising act, so independent has it become from the need to remove liquid waste.

It is also independent, curiously enough, of male virility. Male dogs that have been castrated before reaching puberty will start to cock their legs at the same age as those that are fully sexually active. So, although it is typically an adult masculine activity, it does not seem to be related to the levels of testosterone present, as might be expected. But although it may not be *caused* by the presence of sex hormones, it will certainly leave messages about the sexual condition of the dogs concerned, because sex hormones are excreted in the urine. Also present are special, personal secretions from the male's accessory glands, giving each scent deposit the quality of an identity label.

Three reasons have been given as to why males should cock their legs rather than squat. First, and perhaps most important, is the need to keep the scent signals as fresh as possible. Placing them on the ground makes them more vulnerable to disturbance than 'hanging them up' on vertical features. Second, it brings the scent-stains up to the nose level of other dogs, making them both more conspicuous as odour-spots and also more accessible to sniffing. Third, it helps to inform other dogs, and to remind the urinators themselves, of where the scent-messages are located. A dog can be observed approaching an isolated post or tree from a great distance, just to sniff at it and then cock its leg. In other words, the selection of vertical land-marks helps to restrict the number of places where scents can be found.

A by-product of this male system of scent-marking is that it also makes it easy for one dog to identify the gender of another at a distance, simply by watching the silhouette of its body when it pauses to urinate. This information may then be acted upon in making decisions about whether or not to approach.

What exactly are the messages transmitted by the scent left on the landmarks chosen for leg-cocking urination? Several suggestions have been put forward and they are probably all correct: the first idea is that the message is to the dog itself. By leaving a personal scent all around its patrolled home region, the dog makes the area its own. When it returns it will smell itself and will know that it is on familiar ground. We feel at home inside our own houses because they are full of our personal belongings and bric-à-brac.

The dog feels at home because it has plastered land-marks of its territory with its odour 'belongings'. The second idea is that the message is for other dogs, telling them of the sexual condition and territorial presence of this particular dog. It can serve to bring the sexes together or to warn off other males from trespassing. Against this, it has been argued that males are fascinated by other dogs' smells and never shy away from their scent-marks in fear and trembling. But the fact that these marks are not directly threatening does not mean that they fail to label the area as 'occupied'. Thirdly, a special modification of this last idea is that the real basis of the scent-marking is one of

time-sharing. If, in the wild state, groups of dogs are to live near one another with the minimum of conflict, it helps to know when and how often neighbouring groups pass by. Since the strength and quality of the scent-marks depend on their freshness, it is possible to gauge the frequency with which other dogs patrol the area. Time-sharing of particular zones can then become possible, with groups avoiding one another rather than becoming involved in direct and possibly damaging confrontations.

Studies of free-roaming village dogs reveal that they spend as much as two to three hours every day checking all the scent-marks in their territory. This involves them in daily expeditions of several miles, with every scent-stained landmark along the way being carefully sniffed and read for its latest messages. Although this means the expenditure of a great deal of time and effort, it nevertheless gives every dog in a particular village a complete dog-map of the area, with information about local canine population size, movements, sexual condition and identity.

Female dogs are generally believed never to cock their legs, but this is not strictly true. About a quarter of all females will raise one back leg when urinating, but the way this is done differs from the male's action. In the female leg-raising, one of the back legs is lifted up underneath her body, rather than stretched out to one side. The result is that her urine still falls on the ground rather than on a vertical surface. Occasionally she will overcome this problem by performing an awkward-looking handstand posture, walking backwards up a post or wall and then urinating with both legs off the ground. Very rarely she may even cock her leg in the male fashion.

VII

WHY DOES A DOG SCRATCH THE GROUND AFTER DEFECATING?

EVERY DOG-OWNER HAS OBSERVED THE WAY IN WHICH a dog – especially a male dog – will perform several powerful ground-scratching movements after it has completed its act of defecation. It moves slightly away from the exact spot on which the faeces have been deposited and then, with strong backward movements of forelegs, and, in particular, the hind legs, it scrapes the ground repeatedly before walking off. More rarely, scraping behaviour is performed after urination.

The original explanation of this action was that it is a remnant of the time when the wild ancestors of dogs used to cover their faeces like cats. It was thought that domestication had eroded the efficiency of the action, leaving it now no more than a useless vestige of a once hygienic procedure. There is no truth in this, however, because recent observation of wolves in their natural state has revealed that they, too, perform the same kind of scraping actions. There has been no 'decay' due to domestication.

Another suggestion was that the dogs were attempting to scatter their faeces, widening the area over which they were leaving their personal scent. Some species of animals do indeed indulge in scattering their droppings, the hippopotamus, for instance, having a specially flattened tail that is flicked back and forth like the proverbial fan to scatter its scented dung far and wide. However, although dogs always scrape their feet very close to their faeces, they always seem to avoid touching them.

This leaves two possible explanations. First, it has been noticed that in the wild state, when wolves scratch the earth, they disturb the soil and the ground litter over an area of several feet. This leaves a conspicuous visual marker alongside the odour signal of the faeces. Dogs scratching on a pavement or on other hard urban surfaces, where so many owners walk them today, may make little visual impact with their foot-scraping, but that is simply their bad luck. In a more natural setting, their scratching would leave a much more impressive visual signal.

Second, it has been pointed out that the only efficient sweat glands on a dog's body are those between its toes, and the animal may merely be adding yet another personal odour to the one already present in the faeces. We may not find this idea convincing, because although our human noses can detect canine faeces all too easily, our response to the smell of canine foot-sweat is non-existent. In the odour-rich world of dogs, however, it is possible that this additional form of scent-marking has its own particular messages to impart, which provide further fascination to the canine obsession for taking a walk. In all probability, both the scent factor and the visual factor play a role, when the dog makes its scraping action in a natural environment.

VIII

DO DOGS SHOW REMORSE?

MANY DOG-OWNERS CLAIM THAT THEY HAVE observed their dogs behaving in a guilty fashion when they have done something wrong, as if trying to apologize for their misdeeds. Is this a case of people endowing dogs with human emotions they do not really possess, or are canines truly capable of feelings of remorse?

The most obvious explanation of an unusually submissive display by a dog that has 'broken the rules' is that it is responding to the rising anger of its human owner. Dogs are excellent at detecting 'intention movements' – those tell-tale first signs that something is about to happen. The dog-owner who is about to express his anger may tense his body before he actually shouts at the dog, and the animal is capable of reading this tension and behaving accordingly. So if it starts to approach submissively before it has been reprimanded, it may simply be making a correct guess as to what is about to come. A direct reaction of this sort cannot be called remorse. Simple fear is enough to explain it.

Some dog-owners, however, insist that they have seen their dogs behaving submissively even before the 'crime' has been discovered. For example, a dog shut in a room alone for too long eventually makes a mess on the carpet, or, out of boredom, chews up a slipper or a glove or does some other damage in the course of keeping itself occupied. If it has learnt in the past that such behaviour is forbidden, it may then greet its owner's return with an unusually friendly but rather strangely submissive display. If the owner has not yet had a chance to see the damage that has been done, there is no way that his behaviour can give any clues to the dog about 'impending anger'. So the behaviour of the dog is an independent appeasement action caused by an understanding that it has done something 'wrong'. This means that, in effect, a dog is capable of showing remorse.

Similar behaviour has been observed in wolves. A group of hungry captive wolves was thrown a large piece of meat in such a way that it was caught by one of the weaker animals. This low-ranking individual grabbed the meat and rushed off into a corner with it. When approached by the dominant wolves, it snarled and snapped at them, defending its prize.

In wolf society one of the laws of social behaviour is that ownership of a piece of food overrules dominance relations. In other words, no matter how high or low your social status, once you have a piece of meat in your mouth it is yours. Even the most powerful member of the pack cannot take it from you then. There is what has been called an 'ownership zone', which extends about twelve inches

from the mouth of each feeding wolf, and inside that zone no trespassing is permitted. (Dog-owners will have noticed a similar phenomenon. Even the lowliest member of a group of pet dogs will snap out and attack the others if they come too close when it is chewing on a piece of meat or a bone.) In the case of this hungry wolf-pack, the dominant animals were desperate to take the meat away from the weaker animal but refrained from doing so. He ate about half the meat and then, in an unguarded moment, the remainder of it was stolen when he was not looking. The dominant ones then ate their fill. After this was all over, the weak animal actively approached the dominant ones and offered them a cringing display of submissive behaviour. Each of the 'top wolves' in turn received this treatment, despite the fact that they were showing no threat or outward aggression of any kind to the low-status individual. It was as though the meat-grabber felt compelled to apologize for its earlier behaviour and to make it quite clear that it was not making a serious bid for a high-status role.

Although dog-owners may be familiar with such actions and take them for granted, they do nevertheless reveal a remarkably complex appreciation of social rules on the part of the dog. It is an appreciation that is lacking in many other species and which is directly related to the more social pack-life of their wild ancestors.

IX

WHY DO WE SPEAK OF 'DOG-DAYS'?

THE DOG-DAYS COVER THE HOTTEST PERIOD OF summer, from July 3rd to August 11th, when the weather is sultry and the air stifling. People often puzzle over the connection between the time of great heat and the dog. This is not surprising, as the link is obscure. It dates back to Roman times, when it was believed that Sirius, the Dogstar, added its heat to that of the sun during this period, creating the exceptionally high temperatures. They called this period of the year *dies caniculares*, or days of the dog. Although it is of course nonsense to suggest that the Dogstar adds to the sun's heat in summer, since the star is 540,000 times as distant as the sun, the Romans did at least guess correctly about its temperature. We now know that it gives a reading of 10,000°C, which is roughly twice that of the sun.

Because people were ignorant of this ancient origin of the term dog-days, they later assumed incorrectly that it referred to the time of year when the heat was so oppressive that it drove dogs mad, causing them to rush about in a frenzy. Some dogs may indeed have suffered from the heat, especially in the Mediterranean region, but their association with the term was a mere afterthought.

HOW DO DOGS INVITE PLAY?

IN MOST SPECIES OF MAMMALS PLAYFULNESS FADES AS individuals become adult. Two notable exceptions to this rule are dogs and people. During the course of evolution we ourselves became 'juvenile apes', retaining our childhood curiosity and our playfulness right through our adult lives. It was this change that gave us our remarkable inventiveness and it is at the heart of our amazing success story. So it is not surprising that the animal most favoured as our close companion should share with us an extended playfulness.

Just as we are juvenile apes, so dogs are juvenile wolves. As adults, all breeds of domestic dogs remain unusually playful, even after they have reached an advanced age. One of the problems they have to face is how to indicate to other dogs, or to people, that they are in a playful mood. Since play often involves mock fighting and mock fleeing, it is crucial to make it clear that a particular action is only in fun and is not to be taken seriously. This is done by performing special play-invitation displays.

The most popular of these 'let's play' signals is the play-bow, in which the dog dramatically lowers the front half of its body while keeping its rear end raised. Its front legs are in a 'sitting sphinx' position, so that its chest touches or nearly touches the ground, in contrast with its hind legs which are fully stretched vertically. In this position the play-ful dog stares intently at its companion and makes small forward-jerking movements as if saying 'let's go, let's go'. If the companion responds, there follows either a play-chase or a play-flight. Because of the way this chasing or fleeing has been initiated with the special play-signal, the chasing never leads to a real attack and the fleeing never ends with the retreating dog being seriously bitten. In fact, chaser and escaper may switch roles time and again, taking it in turns to be pursuer and pursued, and the speed with which they switch reveals that they are not experiencing moods of real aggression or fear, but are merely acting the parts. Running in wide circles is typical of this type of play.

In origin, it has been suggested that the play-bow is a modified stretching movement. It is certainly very similar to the kind of leg-stretching that is seen when a dog wakes up and prepares to become active. The idea is that, by making a 'stretch' display, the animal indicates that it is relaxed and that the attacking and fleeing which are about to start are therefore not serious. But a more likely explanation is simply that the bow is a frozen intention-movement of prancing away, rather like the crouched posture adopted by a track athlete when waiting for the starter's gun.

There are several other typical canine play-invitation signals. One is the so-called play-face, an expression which is the canine equivalent of the human smile and which has similar components. The lips are pulled back horizontally but not vertically. The mouth-line therefore gets longer, with the mouth-corners retreating towards the ears. The jaws are slightly opened but there is no attempt to show off the front teeth. In a way, this is the opposite of the snarl of an angry dog, where the mouth-corners come forward and the nose wrinkles upwards to reveal all the front teeth. A dog showing a play-face is completely non-aggressive.

Other incitements to join in play include nudging, pawing and offering. Nudging with the nose is derived from infantile pushing movements made by the pups feeding at their mother's teats. Pawing at or towards a companion to start them playing is also derived from infantile feeding behaviour. A playful dog may simply sit, staring at a companion, and then make downward swipes of one front paw in the air, as if beckoning.

The 'offering' signal is a way of teasing someone into play. The dog brings an object, such as a ball or a stick, and lies facing its companion with its offering placed on the ground between its front feet. The moment you attempt to pick it up, the dog snatches it with its teeth and scampers off. If you chase the dog it has succeeded – you have become embroiled in a play pattern. If you stop, the offering will be made again.

Sometimes a very high-spirited dog – typically one that has been shut up for a while and is now released on to an open space – performs an elaborate prancing and whirling display, as a signal that play should begin. The movements – running, twisting, leaping, jumping and zigzagging – are characteristically over-exaggerated. Interspersed among them may be brief play-bows, quickly performed and abandoned as the playful dog dashes off yet again on its crazily conspicuous prancing runs. This type of behaviour is sometimes used by wild wolves to lure their prey. By dancing about in a strange fashion, they fascinate their victims which can then be approached more easily. In the last century in North America, this luring strategy was exploited by human duck-hunters. They encouraged their dogs, usually Poodles, to leap about playfully on an open place. Upon seeing this, wild ducks could not resist coming closer to investigate what was going on, and that was their undoing. Catching ducks this way was called 'tolling' and the dogs were called 'tollers'. The fact that even ducks were attracted reveals just how inviting the canine play-inciting actions have become during the entire course of evolution.

Some young dogs are, however, too scared to join in bouts of play with their elders. Adults find this frustrating and will go to great lengths to provoke their junior companions. One strategy employed in this particular context is the 'reassurance display'. A dominant animal deliberately flops down on the ground near to the timid juveniles and rolls on to its back in the full passive-dog posture. This momentary acting-out of low status makes the young ones feel more important and they bravely come close. Then play can begin. This form of interaction can also be observed when a very large adult dog wants to play with a very small one. The submissive posture of the larger animal is highly effective at putting the little one at its ease and permitting a play sequence to blossom.

For dogs to play well as adults it is crucial that they should have enjoyed playing with litter-mates when young. It is during the first few months of life that puppies discover the need to perform what is called the 'soft-bite'. At first, when they start wrestling with one another they do not inhibit their bites and their sharp teeth cause yelps and whines of pain. But when they realize that hard biting stops the playful rough-and-tumble, they quickly learn to inhibit the strength of their jaw movements. Dogs that have been isolated when young and deprived of this puppy play-phase sometimes become trouble-makers as adults. Lacking the soft-bite, they hurt their play-mates and real fighting can then erupt. Such dogs become pests in public parks where dogs gather to play.

XI

WHY DO MALE DOGS LIKE HAVING THEIR CHESTS SCRATCHED?

A FAMOUS DOG-TRAINER ONCE REDUCED A STUDIO audience to uncontrollable laughter during a television programme by announcing that it is extremely important to scratch a male between his legs. She was, of course, discussing the best way to please a male dog when touching it. There are, in fact, seven different ways in which we make amicable physical contact with our dogs, and there are some intriguing hidden factors operating in the mode of contact we choose.

Scratching a male dog's chest, down between his front legs, is indeed very pleasing to him. The reason is not hard to find. When he mounts the female and makes pelvic thrusts, his chest rubs against her back in a rhythmic way. By rubbing him there with our hand, we automatically ring these pleasure bells at the back of his mind. This particular form of contact is therefore especially useful when we want to praise a male dog. Tickling or scratching behind the ears of any dog also seems to give them pleasure. This too is sexual in its significance, because ear-licking, sniffing and nibbling are part of the preliminaries of canine courtship.

Gentle pushing away of a playful dog excites it greatly. This is because, inadvertently, we have joined in a play-fight. The playful dog immediately leaps forward again, urging us to push once more, and the game can continue and develop into play biting, with the dog gently grabbing our hand in its jaws, or allowing us to grab its jaws with our hand. Providing all the movements from both sides are gentle enough, this type of playful interaction serves to strengthen the bond between owner and dog, just as it does between puppy and puppy.

Patting a dog is perhaps the most common form of physical contact between animal and owner. The pat has a special significance for us, because it is the action we use when embracing friends and loved ones of our own species. So to pat a dog's back unconsciously makes us feel that we are being intimate with a very close friend. For the dog the reward is different. Dogs do not pat one another on the back, so what can this action mean to them? The answer seems to be that they interpret the pat as a 'nudging' or 'nosing' contact. This is something which puppies do to the bellies of their mothers, and which subordinate dogs do to dominant ones. So for our pet dogs this type of contact must be immensely rewarding. To them it must be read as a submissive act on our part, but since they know that we are the dominant members of their pack, they can only interpret it in one way: as a reassurance display. When top dogs wish to reassure inferior dogs, they sometimes approach them in a mock-submissive posture, to put them at their ease. This is how patting must seem to our dogs.

Dogs with long, silky coats sometimes make us switch from patting to stroking, as if we are handling a cat rather than a dog. This action has less impact, but the gentle grooming effect may remind the animal of its earliest days with its mother, when it was a tiny puppy licked by the bitch's huge tongue.

Children, in particular, love cuddling dogs and the animals are extremely tolerant of such behaviour. The reason why they accept this type of contact so readily is because it reminds them of their days with their litter-mates, when they were all clumping together in a heap to feel secure and warm, or when their mother wrapped her large body around them in the nest.

Finally, many dogs enjoy having the sides of their heads rubbed, especially along the jawline. In this contact the human is offering the animal a comfort action it often performs for itself. Dogs with mild irritations in the mouth region, especially the teeth, like to rub the sides of their heads against hard edges of furniture. Being scratched or rubbed there by their owners does the work for them and they appreciate it.

What dogs are not so keen on is the full wash-and-brush-up they must endure if they are prize show dogs. Hours of careful bathing and hairdressing are more than a dog can understand. It takes grooming beyond the level of importance that it holds in canine social life. But, being subordinate in their households, they have little choice and endure it as stoically as if being bullied by a dominant dog. Human beings are fortunate in having such a co-operative and sociable species as their closest animal companion.

XII

HOW DOES A SUBMISSIVE DOG ACT?

THE SHORT ANSWER IS: LIKE A PUPPY. WEAK ADULTS IN many species of animals adopt juvenile postures or perform infantile actions when they are threatened by a dominant individual. If they lack the courage to match threat with counter-threat and risk engaging in a serious dispute, they resort to the animal equivalent of waving a white flag. The problem is to find an action that will switch off the aggressive mood of the attacker. One way to do this is to adopt a posture that is the opposite of the threat display. If in one species the aggressor lowers his head ready to charge, the submissive animal raises his head; if in another species the aggressor raises his head making himself seem bigger, the submissive one meekly lowers his own. If the aggressor erects his fur, the submissive one flattens his fur; if the aggressor stands tall, the submissive one crouches. And so on. But this is only one of two basic types of animal appeasement strategy.

The second solution is to arouse in the aggressor a mood which conflicts strongly with its hostility and thereby subdues it. Adults usually have strong inhibitions about attacking the young of their own species, so that a sudden display of pseudo-puppy behaviour by an adult dog can have the desired effect of blocking an assault.

Dogs use two devices, one for moments of passive submission and another for active submission. In passive displays, the weak animal has no choice. The aggressor approaches and threatens. The subordinate individual crouches low, trying to appear as small as possible and then, if this fails to stop the assault, it rolls over on to its back with its paws held limply in the air. In this position it may emit a little jet of urine. This copies the behaviour of tiny puppies when the mother approaches to lick them and thereby stimulate urination. (When they are only a few days old they will not urinate by themselves. The bitch has to turn them over with her nose and then repeatedly lick their bellies to start the urine flowing.) By volunteering such a posture, a submissive adult transmits the most powerful infantile signal available in canine body language. And it usually succeeds, like magic, in dissipating the aggressor's hostility.

Active submission requires different tactics. If a weak animal wishes to approach a dominant one it cannot do so lying on its back. It must find some other appeasement display to signal that its intentions are totally non-hostile. It does this by employing another action performed by puppies towards their elders. This can best be described as the crouching face-lick. When the puppies are a month old they start begging for food from the adults. They do this by reaching up with their snouts and nuzzling the adult animal's mouth. They lick its face and nudge its head until

it disgorges some morsels of food. Active submission follows the same pattern. The problem here is that the subordinate animal is now roughly the same size as the dominant one. If it simply approaches the 'top dog' and licks its face, the movement will appear too assertive. To avoid this, it lowers its body into a semi-crouch. This takes it down to the appropriate 'puppy-level'. It can then *raise* its head up towards the dominant one's mouth and, in so doing, re-create the necessary infantile attitude.

By adopting this juvenile food-begging posture, a subordinate adult can come close to any dog in its social group without risking attack. It enables the animals to keep near one another without repeated quarrels erupting.

DOES A BEATEN DOG
OFFER ITS THROAT TO ITS ATTACKER?

NO, IT DOES NOT. THE REASON FOR ASKING THIS question is that the famous Austrian naturalist Konrad Lorenz made a great deal of the observation that when a savagely aggressive wolf (or dog) has beaten its rival and is just about to bite it to death, the weaker animal quickly twists its head to display its vulnerable throat. Its jugular vein is exposed to the great fangs of the attacker and it is suddenly and deliberately at the mercy of its assailant. The assailant immediately accepts this canine version of 'throwing in the towel' or 'showing the white flag' and inhibits its savage bite, acknowledging the surrender with chivalry. This gentlemanly behaviour impressed Lorenz and he developed a whole theory around it.

Unfortunately it was based on a complete misreading of canine behaviour. What Lorenz had seen was one animal turning its head away and standing stiffly still, while another sniffed and nipped at its muzzle. He assumed that the snapping animal was the dominant aggressor, which wanted to bite the other but was inhibited from doing so by the 'showing of a vulnerable spot'. In reality the roles were the other way around. The snapper was the subordinate animal performing its display of active submission (the display borrowed from the food-begging actions of puppies trying to persuade a parent to regurgitate food). The animal stiffly turning its head away was the dominant one, responding to the weaker animal's submissive display.

On the very rare occasions when fighting does become really serious, there is no 'showing of the throat'. The only hope for a beaten dog is to flee as fast and as far as possible. Otherwise it may be killed. This is how certain young males become outcasts from packs of feral dogs (or wild wolves). If they have made a serious challenge and been beaten by the dominant dog, they must leave the group and try to survive on their own, or join up with outcasts from other groups to form a new pack.

For the pet dog in the home these aspects of canine violence have little meaning. Their top dog is their owner and he is too dominant to engage in a serious dispute. So for them there is a life of friendly submission and peace and quiet ... until the postman arrives. As a stranger he is seen as a member of another pack and demands an immediate challenge. If the unfortunate man has happened to read one of Lorenz's books and offers his jugular to the dog racing down the path towards him, he will be in for something of a shock.

WHY DOES A FRIGHTENED DOG PUT ITS TAIL BETWEEN ITS LEGS?

EVERYONE KNOWS THE MEANING OF THIS TAIL POSTURE, but why has it evolved its particular role in the body language of dogs? Why should a tail-down position be linked with fear, insecurity, subordination, appeasement and displays of low status, while a tail-up position is the sign of dominance and high status?

The answer lies not in the tail itself, but in what is beneath it. By lowering the tail and then curling it tightly between the hind legs, the cringing dog is effectively cutting off the scent signals from its anal region. When two high-ranking dogs meet, they proudly raise their tails high to expose their anal zones to close examination. Since the anal glands carry personal scents that identify the individual dogs, the tail-between-the-legs action is the canine equivalent of insecure human beings hiding their faces.

For a single pet dog living with a human family this display is of no great importance, but wherever there is a social grouping of dogs in which relative status and rank order are important, it is a vital signal that protects the weaker members of the group from the stronger. Inevitably, it is particularly important in wolf society in the wild. A subordinate wolf can be observed lowering its tail as it approaches a dominant individual, tucking the tail tightly between its back legs as it passes close to the 'top wolf' and then raising it again as it moves on out of range.

There is an intriguing difference between domestic dogs and their wild ancestors in connection with these tail displays. On the tails of all wolves (but not dogs) there is a special pre-caudal gland, which can be observed as a dark spot about three inches from the base of the tail. Surrounded by black-tipped stiffened hairs, this small skin gland is made up of a group of modified sebaceous glands which exude a fatty secretion. Like the anal glands, it is solely concerned with scent-signalling and its positioning on the outside of the tail is significant. Being placed where it is, it provides a scent-sniffing location that acts like a mimic anal zone. If a wolf approaches a companion to sniff its rump, it will find one kind of scent gland if the tail is up (the anal gland) and another, in the same position, if the tail is down (the pre-caudal tail gland). This means that the scent-signalling of the wolf is more complex than that of the domestic dog.

Why the dog has abandoned this tail-gland signal is not at all clear. All of the other changes that have taken place during the 10,000 year development of the dog from the wolf have been deliberately selected by human dog-breeders to improve this or that quality in their animals, ending up with the many distinctive breeds we have today. But the function of the tail gland of the wolf has only been discussed in very recent times, so it is hard to see how it could

could have become the focus of breeding trends in previous centuries. Yet it must have been eliminated at a very early stage because its loss appears to be complete in all dog breeds. It is the one difference between wolves and dogs that remains a complete mystery at the present time.

A final point about the tail-up and tail-down displays of dogs and wolves: although the primary function is undoubtedly the modification of scent-signals, a secondary, visual message has also become important. It is possible for any animal watching from a distance, as an encounter takes place, to see at a glance which of the two 'performers' is dominant and which subordinate, simply by their silhouettes. A brief look is all that is needed to check whether there has been any change in status relations and whether a weaker animal is perhaps, at last, starting to challenge a stronger one.

XV

WHY DO WE CURE A HANGOVER WITH THE 'HAIR OF THE DOG'?

THE SUGGESTION IS THAT A SMALL DRINK ON THE morning after a drunken night out will help to cure the hangover. The fallacious idea that the very thing which caused the pain will also cure it is paralleled in an early cure for dog-bites. In an eighteenth-century volume on 'The Treatment of Canine Madness' the author comments that 'The hair of the dog that gave the wound is advised as an application to the part injured.' This was, in all seriousness, thought to help in the healing of the wound, but it is doubtful whether today's drunken reveller really believes that the 'hair of the dog that bit him' will do more than mask the pain.

XVI

HOW DOES A 'TOP DOG' BEHAVE?

MOST OF THE BEHAVIOUR THAT OWNERS SEE IN THEIR dogs is friendly or submissive, because it is the human members of the 'pack' that are the truly dominant ones. But where several dogs live together it is possible to observe the way in which the 'top dog' treats its subordinates.

If the dominance of the senior dog is challenged, it will perform a threat display in an attempt to subdue the upstart without having to resort to force. Essentially the display does two things: it makes the dominant animal look larger and stronger, and it demonstrates the animal's eager readiness to plunge into the attack, should an attack be necessary. This is usually enough to scare off any rival.

The threat display is made up of ten characteristic elements, each of which contributes its special signal to the enemy:

1   The teeth are bared by pulling the upper lip up and the lower lip down. This exposes the canines and the incisors, and indicates that the threatening animal is ready to sink its fangs into the enemy.

2   The mouth is open, showing that the dog is ready to clamp down with its jaws.

3   The mouth-corners are drawn forward. This is the opposite of the friendly, playful and submissive facial expressions, in all of which the mouth-corners are pulled back towards the ears. This element of the threat display makes it clear that the dog is neither friendly, nor playful, nor submissive.

4   The ears are erect and forward-pointing. Even in flop-eared breeds there is a brave attempt to assume this position, which tells the enemy that the dog is fully alert and listening intently for any tell-tale sound of fear or aggression. It also demonstrates that the aggressor is so confident that it feels no need to protect the ears by flattening them.

Those are the facial expression elements of threat. The rest of the body is also transmitting signals:

5   The tail is held high, in contrast to the submissive tail-between-the-legs posture. This tail-up posture exposes the anal region with its special odours. These scents successfully identify the dog (while the tail-down dog tries to hide its identity). They let the weaker animal know precisely who it is dealing with.

The body of the threatening animal is also made to look as big as possible:

6   There are special erectile patches of hair around the shoulders and on the back and rump. This combined mane-and-crest stands on end when the most intense form of threat display is performed.

7   At the same time, the legs are fully stretched and the whole body suddenly seems awesomely more massive and powerful.

8   The effect is heightened by an intense, unwavering stare.

9   A deep rumbling growl is uttered.

10 The body is so tense that the tail trembles, in its bolt-upright position.

This fearsome sight is enough to make most rivals cringe and slink away. It is used in serious confrontations where the dominant animal feels there is a real challenge to its high status. At other times, when the mood is more relaxed, a dominant dog may offer occasional reminders of its power, using other types of display. One is the broadside ritual in which it deliberately pushes itself up against a weaker dog, which may be standing or lying down. The top dog positions itself across the subordinate, as if trying to block its path, and stiffly remains there long enough to give the message 'I control your movements.' Alternatively, it may perform the mounting ritual, in which it rears up and places its front legs on the lesser animal's back or shoulders. This is the first move towards mounting for copulation, but it is used here in a totally non-sexual context. It is the canine equivalent of saying 'up yours'.

The other ways in which the dominant animal lets its subordinates know who is boss are the spring-threat and the ambush-threat. In the first, the dog makes the intention movement of springing at the enemy, but without bothering to carry it through. In the second, the dog crouches as if in an ambush, but makes its position quite conspicuous to its rival. In both cases the subordinate gets the message very quickly and reacts accordingly.

All these different threats remind the inferior dogs of the high status of the top dog. But he does not have to perform them very often, if the group of dogs lives together. In fact, most of the time the relations within the group are very organized and friendly. In a species where co-operative hunting was the key to successful evolution, it is essential that top dogs (or top wolves) are not too overbearing.

XVII

WHY DOES A DOG BURY A BONE?

TO UNDERSTAND WHY DOMESTIC DOGS SOMETIMES bury bones it is necessary to take a look at the way in which wolves hunt in the wild. Small prey, such as mice, are stalked, chased and pounced upon by single wolves working for themselves. The pounce traps the prey under the front feet. It is then seized and quickly bitten several times, after which it is rapidly gobbled down. Slightly larger prey, such as rabbits, are treated in the same way. If a prey animal of this size proves difficult, it may be shaken vigorously, but usually a few bites are all that is needed to subdue it. Medium-sized animals, such as sheep or small deer, are killed by throat-bites. Death takes only a few seconds. With all such animals, from mice to sheep, there is no need to store food by burying it. Even a small deer can be consumed quickly by only a few wolves. Each adult wolf is capable of swallowing as much as twenty pounds of meat in a single sitting, and as much as forty-four pounds in a period of twenty-four hours.

Only with very large prey, such as big deer, cattle or horses, do the wolves have a serious surplus of food. Even in such cases, however, they usually leave the carcass where it lies after they have eaten their fill, and return to it later. If the wolf-pack is small, however, and consists of only a few adult animals, they may take the precaution of tearing off large hunks of meat and burying them under the ground. This protects the food from scavengers, especially birds such as crows, ravens and vultures. In hot summer weather it also protects the meat from flies and maggots. Typically the burying takes place near the kill, but sometimes the hunks of meat are carried back to the den and hidden there.

The burying action consists of digging a hole with the front feet while still clasping the meat in the jaws. When the cavity is big enough, the wolf simply opens its jaws and lets the meat drop into it. It then uses its snout to push earth back on top of the cache. Unlike a cat, it never employs its front feet to fill in a hole that it has dug. Once the hole is covered over, the animal makes a few pressing-down movements with its snout and then wanders off. It returns the following day, digs up the meat with its front feet, grabs it in its jaws, gives one powerful shake to remove the earth that is clinging to its hoard, and then settles down to eating it.

Returning to the domestic dog, it is now easy to see what conditions must be present to encourage it to bury food. In the first instance, there must be a food surplus. A hungry dog would, like its wolf ancestors, eat everything it could. Only if there was something left over that could not be eaten would it be carried into the garden and buried. Commercial dog food, even in homes where animals are

73

overfed by their owners, is impossible to carry and hold in the jaws while digging a hole. So dogs fed only soft food in dog-bowls will never have the opportunity to bury anything. But if they are given large bones they do, at last, have something they can carry and hide in a hole.

The reason why bones are so popular as burying objects is that, even if the dogs in question are not overfed and have no real food surplus, a large bone, which is impossible to break up and eat, has about it the essential quality of a food object that 'cannot be eaten now'. It is this 'left-over' quality that is able to persuade even a hungry dog to bury it.

Some pet dogs, overfed with soft foods, can be seen performing a strange remnant of food-burying. They know the dish of surplus food is good food, but they are not hungry, so they attempt to bury the whole dish in a corner of a room. The burying actions are only fragmentary in such instances. Usually the animal does no more than make 'covering-up' movements with its nose. These actions often push the dish along the floor, but have no other effect and the dog soon gives up. This animal is telling its owner is that it has been given too much food. Rather than leave it to imaginary scavengers, the animal goes through the motions of saving the food for a later occasion.

XVIII

HOW OFTEN DO DOGS FEED?

MOST DOG-OWNERS GIVE THEIR DOGS TWO FEEDS A day and this, with fresh water, is sufficient to keep them healthy, providing the food is varied and not totally restricted to meat. Wild dogs and wolves consume a certain amount of vegetable food when they gobble down the entrails of their herbivorous prey, and domestic dogs have a similar nutritional need. But a recent trend to give pet dogs vegetarian diets is even worse than all-meat diets. The dog is an omnivore, like man, and needs a balanced menu.

Some owners have the strange idea that on one day each week their dogs must be made to fast. This food-deprivation regime is based on the fact that, in the wild, wolves can go for considerable periods without any food whatever. Fourteen days without eating has been recorded in harsh environments. These fast periods are then followed by massive gorging and rapid digestion when a large prey is finally brought down and killed.

Because this feeding pattern occurs in nature it is thought to be a preferred way of eating, but this is not the case. Given a richer environment with plentiful prey, wolves always eat several times daily. The fact that they can survive on a gorging diet should not be taken as a guide for domestic dog-feeding regimes. It is worth remembering that, back in our primeval hunting days, our ancient ancestors were themselves surviving on a gorge-and-fast diet for much of the time. But although we could return to this feeding pattern today without killing ourselves, we thrive much better on several meals a day, and the same is true for the dog.

WHY IS A SHEEPDOG SO GOOD AT HERDING SHEEP?

THE AMAZING SKILLS OF SHEPHERDS AND THEIR DOGS during televised sheepdog trials have fascinated large audiences. There seems to be an uncanny, almost telepathic relationship between man and animal. But, although the performances are truly remarkable, they are easy enough to explain in terms of canine hunting behaviour. The working sheepdog is simply drawing on instincts inherited from its wolf ancestry and modifying its ancient hunting pattern to suit the needs of the shepherd. This becomes clearer by looking briefly at the way a wolf-pack behaves when it is stalking.

To be encircled by a pack of wolves is a memorable experience. Even with a well-fed pack you have known since they were cubs, there is an eerie sensation as the animals fan out around you. You know what it must feel like to be a hunted deer about to die. In the same moment you understand in a flash what a sheepdog is doing when it is herding a flock of sheep. As it runs this way and that, it is trying to act like a one-dog wolf-pack. The odds are heavily stacked against it. Instead of one prey and a whole group of predators, there is one lone predator and a whole group of prey. The poor sheepdog must do the work of ten wolves, and it is little wonder that these amazing dogs die much younger than other breeds, so exhausted are they by their absorbing work.

The reason why sheepdogs push themselves to the limits is that as soon as they have crouched down in one place, eyeing the sheep with a fixed expression, they notice that, to their lupine horror, there is no wolf to the left of them and no wolf to the right either. They alone constitute the primeval encirclement. So they scurry this way and that, running and crouching, running and crouching, trying to be a whole circle of wolves all at once. The wolf instincts inside them will settle for nothing less.

The hunting strategy they are acting out is based on four inborn 'instructions'. The first says: when you have singled out a prey, you will approach it to approximately the same distance as your pack-mates. The second says: you will position yourself equidistant from the wolf on your left and the one on your right. Put together, these two rules automatically produce a circle of wolves around the prey. If you have ever watched a pack forming a circle around your own body, you will see how these two rules interact. When the group first sights you and advances, it may be quite tightly clustered together. Then, as it approaches, each wolf moves apart from its nearest companions and continues to spread out, but keeping a set distance from you. Encirclement, which looks so elegant and complex, is therefore really quite a simple manoeuvre. The sheepdog, as it dashes from one position to another around a flock of sheep, sets its own 'key distance' from the flock and then proceeds to fill the different stations of its missing pack-mates, one after the other.

A third feature of hunting by a wolf-pack is the ambush element. One particular wolf may take off on its own, separate from the encircling pack, and hide from the prey. Lying still on the ground, it waits as the rest of the group slowly drive the nearly encircled victim towards it. This ambush refinement is also part of the sheepdog's strategy. Sometimes it will run and lie, as if hidden, low on the ground, fixating upon the flock of sheep. At this moment it is the ambusher, but when the flock starts to move, it must then become the whole encircling group again.

A final and crucially important aspect of wolf-hunting is the role of the dominant member of the pack. This 'top wolf' is the one that initiates the various moves and decides on the selection of a particular prey. The other wolves pay great attention to its behaviour and follow its lead. This avoids disagreements which would completely destroy the efficiency of the hunt. For the sheepdog, the shepherd is the 'top wolf', and his commands are therefore readily accepted at moments where decisions have to be made as to how to manipulate the flock of sheep.

There are ten specific instructions which the shepherd gives to his dog. They are as follows:

1   Stop! (Halt whatever you are doing at the moment.)
2   Lie! (Adopt the ambush position and stay quiet and still on the ground, facing the flock and fixating them with a stare.)
3   Go left! (Move to the left of the flock and, if the signal is repeated, continue to circle round them in that direction.)
4   Go right! (The same, but in the opposite direction.)
5   Come here! (Come towards the shepherd from wherever you are.)
6   Come on! (Move closer to the flock, regardless of where they are.)
7   Go back! (Retreat from the flock.)
8   Steady! (Slow down whatever you are doing.)
9   Speed up! (Be quicker at whatever you are doing.)
10   That will do! (Leave the sheep and return to the side of the shepherd.)

With these ten commands, exploiting the wolf-hunting pattern of the dog, the shepherd can create all the subtle and seemingly complex moves he requires from his sheepdog. He transmits the signals by a mixture of whistles, vocal cries and visual arm signals.

Interestingly, the most difficult manoeuvre he has to teach his dogs to perform is to drive the flock *away* from him. This goes against the grain of wolf-hunting, because the dominant wolf (= the shepherd) would never want his subordinates to move the prey away from him in a natural, wild encounter. But even this is possible with sheepdogs, because of their total obedience to their human masters.

WHY DOES A POINTER POINT?

THE POINTER IS A SPECIALIZED BREED OF GUN-DOG that hunts by scent. Once it has detected a hidden prey, it freezes in its tracks and adopts a curious 'pointing' posture. It lowers its head, stretching its neck forward. Its tail sticks out stiffly behind in a horizontal position. And one of its front feet is held up in mid-air as if caught in mid-step. Standing completely still, like a canine statue, the animal will hold this position for ages. Only a slight trembling or quivering, especially of the tail, reveals the great excitement and tension of the moment.

One Pointer, it is claimed, once remained like this for several hours, but in a normal hunt the dog's human companions soon break the spell by firing at the prey as it flees from cover. This releases the dog from its point and the scent-tracking can resume once more.

Sometimes two Pointers are employed as a team. A single animal can show the direction of a hidden prey by the angle of its point, but it cannot indicate the distance. Two Pointers, fixating on the same prey from different directions, provide co-ordinates for the human hunters, telling them both direction and distance, and pin-pointing the unfortunate victim's precise position.

The behaviour of the Pointer on a hunt seems highly artificial, but it is not. When wolves first scent a prey, the leading members of the pack freeze in their tracks and point themselves rigidly in the direction of the scent. The other members of the pack then follow suit, trying to catch the scent themselves. There is a pause, until they have all fixated on the odour of the prey, and then they begin the next phase of their hunting operation. It is this wolf-pause that the Pointer is performing. The only thing that is strange about the dog example is the way the animal extends the 'frozen moment'. It is this prolongation of the action that is the breed specialization, not the point itself.

Setters set in much the same way that Pointers point, the only difference being that when they scent the hidden prey they sit down and remain pointing towards it from their sitting position. The name 'Setter' is just an old-fashioned way of saying 'sitter'.

The action of the Setter seems to be borrowing more from the wolf's ambushing tactics than from its pointing. There are phases of the hunt where one particular wolf will circle round and then lie hidden, waiting for the prey to be driven in its direction. The Setter appears to have 'enlarged' this element of the wolf hunt and made it his breed speciality.

Retrievers that rush after shot prey and bring them back to their human companions are borrowing yet another element from lupine hunting. Wild wolves will return to their dens with food offerings for she-wolves that are

whelping, or for cubs that are too young to take part in the hunt. This helpful food-sharing tendency is the one that has been exploited by generations of dog-breeders to produce the selfless retrieving of the modern gun-dogs of this type.

The same action of returning to the den with food is also the basis of that most popular of dog-games, fetching a thrown stick or ball.

XXI

WHY DO DOGS EAT GRASS?

ALTHOUGH THEY ARE CARNIVORES, BOTH CATS AND dogs occasionally go out into the garden and chew at grass stems. They usually swallow very little and seem to be more interested in the juice from the stems than the solid plant material. In the case of cats, the most recent explanation of this behaviour is that the animals are seeking an important vitamin supplement to their meat diet, in the form of folic acid, which, as its name suggests, is found in foliage. This is probably also true for dogs, but there is another possible explanation.

Some dog-owners notice that, when their pet dogs have visited the lawn to chew up some pieces of grass, this has followed a time of stomach trouble, when the animals' digestion has been upset. After the grass-eating, they often return to the house and then vomit up the grass they have just eaten. Some say this is an indication that they needed more roughage in their diet and that it was this lack of roughage that had upset them in the first place. Taking in the unsuitable grass, they claim, only made matters worse and caused the vomiting.

Another view is that the dogs actually wanted to make themselves sick and instinctively employed grass, which they could not digest, as an emetic. This seems most unlikely, since dogs vomit with great ease.

XXII

HOW WELL CAN DOGS SEE?

DOGS HAVE GOOD EYESIGHT BUT IT DIFFERS FROM ours in several respects. For many years it was believed that they had no colour vision and lived in a totally black and white world. It is now known that this is not the case, but colour is not particularly important to them. Their ratio of rods to cones on the retina of the eye favours the rods much more than ours. Rods are useful for black and white vision in dim light; cones are employed in colour vision. The 'rod-rich' eyes of dogs are therefore specially adapted to a daily cycle which favours dawn and dusk as the periods of major activity. This is called a crepuscular rhythm and is the typical mode for the majority of mammals. Humans are unusually diurnal, and therefore not typical mammals in this respect.

The small number of cones in the eyes of dogs reveals that, although they may not revel in technicolour excitements of the human kind, they must be able to see at least some degree of coloration in their canine landscape. As the great eye expert Gordon Walls so eloquently expressed it, 'To any such semi-nocturnal, rod-rich animal [as a dog] the richest of spectral lights could at best appear only as delicate pastel tints of uncertain identity.' Quite so, but pastel tints are better than none, and it is good to think that our canine companions can share with us at least some colour appreciation as we walk together.

In dim light, dogs have the advantage over us. They have a light-reflecting layer called the *tapetum lucidum* at the back of their eyes, which acts as an image-intensifying device enabling them to make more use of what little illumination there may be. As with cats, which possess the same device, it also makes their eyes shine in the dark.

Another difference between our eyes and theirs is that they are more sensitive to movement and less so to detail. If something stands still when at a good distance from them, it becomes almost invisible. That is why so many prey species 'freeze' and stand motionless when they become alarmed, before trying to flee. Tests have proved that if a dog's owner remains motionless at a distance of 300 yards the animal cannot detect him. If, on the other hand, a shepherd is one mile distant but making bold hand signals, these can be clearly seen by his sheepdog. This sensitivity to movement is, of course, of paramount importance during the long chases when wild dogs are on the hunt. Once the prey is fleeing, the dog's eyes are at their peak of performance.

An additional aid for the hunting dog is its much wider field of vision. A narrow-headed breed like a Greyhound has a visual range of 270°. A more typical dog has a range of 250°. Flat-faced dogs have slightly less. But they all have more than human beings, whose visual field is only 180°.

HOW WELL CAN DOGS HEAR?

WITH SOUNDS OF LOW PITCH A DOG'S EARS HAVE about the same ability as ours. At higher pitch, however, the dog is far superior to us. Our upper range when we are very young is about 30,000 cycles a second. This sinks to 20,000 by the time we are young adults and to only 12,000 by the time we reach retiring age. Dogs have an upper limit of 35,000 to 40,000 cycles per second or, according to recent Russian research, as high as 100,000.

This gives the dog the ability to hear a number of sounds which to us are ultrasonic. If a dog suddenly pricks up its ears and becomes alert, it may be that it has detected the high-pitched squealing of rodents or bats which is totally inaudible to us. The evolution of such sensitive hearing is clearly related to the hunting needs of the ancestors of our domestic dogs, enabling them to detect the presence and movements of rats, mice and other small prey.

As a by-product of this hunting refinement, pet dogs can today react to tiny clues that make their behaviour seem almost telepathic. The best-known examples concern the way in which a man's dog can tell that he is about to arrive home from work. Long before any humans in the house can hear anything unusual, the dog is up and alert, anxiously waiting at the door to greet its master. If the man is returning home on foot, the dog is capable of detecting his particular style of walking and distinguishing it from any other footfalls in the street outside. If the man is driving home, the dog can distinguish the sound of the family car from all other cars passing by on the road.

If these reactions seem difficult to believe, it should be pointed out that in the wild state wolves are capable of hearing a howl from a distance of at least four miles.

HOW SENSITIVE IS A DOG'S NOSE?

IN THE WORLD OF ODOURS AND FRAGRANCES THE human being is an inferior species. Each dog experiences a whole landscape of scents with a subtlety and sensitivity that is as far from our comprehension as higher mathematics is from the dog's. It is difficult to express their superiority in any simple way. Some authorities have said that dogs are 100 times better than us at odour detection; others have put the figure as high as a million times; still others have seriously claimed that it is in the region of 100 million. The truth is that the comparison can only be made in respect of a particular chemical substance. With some sorts of smells, dogs perform little better than us, because the odours in question have no significance for them – the fragrances of flowers, for instance. But with other substances, such as the butyric acid found in sweat, tests have proved beyond doubt that dogs have a responsiveness that is, incredibly, at least one million times better than ours.

Examples of this sweat-detection ability are amazingly impressive. There is the thrown pebble test, in which six men each pick up and throw a pebble as far as they can. A dog is then allowed to sniff the hand of one of these men, after which it successfully finds and retrieves *his* pebble. Just by holding the pebble long enough to throw it the man deposited sufficient sweat for the dog's nose to locate it.

Even more startling is the glass slide test. In this, one of a set of glass slides is touched briefly by a single human fingertip. The slides are then put away carefully for a period of six weeks. When they are taken out again for the experiment the test dog is able to identify the slide that had been touched.

The sweat from human feet seems to be even easier for a dog's nose to detect. Bloodhounds can follow a trail that is as much as four days old and track a subject for up to 100 miles. The scent from human feet is so strong to a dog that it can identify individual feet even in areas where many other feet have trodden, and where shoes have been worn by all concerned.

Because of this ability, made possible because the dog's nose contains 220 million smell-sensitive cells (compared with only five million in humans), canine assistance has been sought in many spheres of detection, some obvious and some less so. We all know that Bloodhounds have been used to trail and track down runaway slaves and, later on, escaped criminals, but it is less well known that dogs have been employed to tell whether pairs of twins are identical or fraternal. Since personal human odour is genetically inherited, identical twins have an identical body scent and dogs cannot tell them apart, whereas fraternal twins have different body scents and can easily be distinguished.

Other tasks for the canine nose have included truffle-hunting, drug-detecting, bomb-searching and the rescuing of avalanche victims buried beneath the snow. The three major drugs, marijuana, cocaine and heroin, all have highly characteristic odours and dogs can sniff them out even when they are carefully sealed and hidden inside objects by smugglers. Even when the drug packets are surrounded with strong perfumes, spices, tobacco or mothballs, this has never fooled the specially trained dogs employed by the drug squad. And dogs trained by bomb-disposal squads have no difficulty in detecting the sulphur in gunpowder or the acid in nitroglycerine. When it comes to distinguishing strange smells, the dog's nose is far more efficient than any machine built by man.

During evolution, the main pressure to develop such astonishing olfactory abilities was, of course, the detection of the prey by scent at a great distance. A wolf has been observed to detect the scent of deer downwind at a distance of one-and-a-half miles. As soon as the odour of the deer reaches the wolf-pack they freeze in their tracks and point their bodies directly towards the prey. After standing stiffly for a moment, verifying the scent, they cluster together, nose-to-nose with their tails wagging excitedly. Then, after about ten to fifteen seconds, they take off towards the deer and the hunt is on. For such animals, especially those living in the frozen north, an acute sense of smell makes the difference between life and death. It is this refined ability that our domestic dogs have inherited.

XXV

WHY DO DOGS SOMETIMES ROLL IN FILTH?

A CANINE ACTIVITY THAT CAUSES SOME DISTRESS TO fastidious owners is their pet's occasional impulse to fling itself down on some vile-smelling object and roll about over it in an abandoned fashion. It may choose a decaying carcass, discovered by chance on a long country walk, or a piece of cow-dung or horse-dung. It has been suggested that this represents the dog's attempt to obliterate a rival odour with its own scent. This interpretation derives from the commonplace observation that, when one dog has cocked its leg and left a urine 'marker' on a scent-post, another dog that passes by later on will seem to feel compelled to mask the previous odour by cocking its own leg and urinating in exactly the same spot.

There is a flaw in this explanation, however. The personal scent left by rubbing against an object is, perhaps not surprisingly, much weaker than that deposited by urination or defecation. The smelly objects on which dogs choose to roll have a particularly powerful odour and, if the function of the action were to mask that odour, then it would make more sense to use urine and faeces in liberal quantities. But such a reaction is never observed. This makes it clear that the rolling dog is certainly not doing its best to mask the strong-smelling substance, and some other explanation has to be sought.

The most likely answer is that the dog is not trying to leave its scent on the object, but just the reverse. By rolling on a cow-pat or the smelly droppings of some other animal, such as a horse or a deer, the dog smothers its coat in the alien smell. This then provides it with the perfect camouflage for hunting these very same animals. Even a stinking carcass, although less like a 'prey-smell', will give the dog a less predatory odour.

A different interpretation sees the 'self-scenting' as a way of conveying information to other members of the dog's social group. If a dog encounters the dung of a possible prey species, rolls in it and then returns from its scouting to join other dogs, it could be telling them of its valuable find and thereby instigating a group hunt. It is certainly true that when a dog has self-scented itself with dung, it becomes immensely interesting to its canine friends (if less so to its human ones). They crowd around and sniff it with great intensity, reading these exciting new odour signals. But whether, in the wild state, this does actually lead to an immediate hunt is not known.

The fact that in laboratory experiments dogs will roll on a wide variety of strong-smelling substances, including lemon rind, perfume, tobacco and rotting garbage, has been mentioned as a weakness in both the camouflage theory and the hunt-incitement theory. The alternative

explanation offered is simply that dogs go into a kind of odour ecstasy when they encounter any very strong-smelling substance, regardless of its particular nature. It is hard to prove or disprove such an idea, so it is of little value. And it is worth remembering that, in the wild state, where this response evolved, the strong smell most likely to be encountered was a heap of dung from a prey species. Carcasses would not lie around long enough to rot and stink. In a truly wild place they would be gobbled up well before that happened. And the other items, such as perfume and tobacco, were not available to the primeval canine ancestors. So the modern dog's reaction to them may have little or no meaning in terms of survival.

XXVI

WHY DO DOGS SOMETIMES DRAG THEIR RUMPS ALONG THE GROUND?

IT HAS BEEN SUGGESTED THAT THIS IS A NORMAL PIECE OF scent-marking behaviour, during which the dogs leave a deposit from their anal glands on the ground. Many other species of carnivores have scent-producing glands in the anal region and some of them do regularly rub these glands against landmarks in their home range. The giant panda is a well-known example, where both male and female frequently patrol their territory, stopping every so often to rub their rumps against a rock or a tree-stump.

With domestic dogs, however, the action of sliding the rump along the ground does not seem to be part of normal, healthy behaviour. Examination of dogs which do this usually reveals that they have impacted anal glands that are causing them irritation or pain. The movement along the ground is primarily concerned, it would seem, not with scent-marking but with seeking relief from discomfort.

The anal glands are two pea-sized organs situated one on either side of the dog's rectum about a quarter of an inch inside the anal opening. Every time the dog defecates, these glands are automatically squeezed, adding a strong-smelling substance to the faeces. There is apparently no variation in this particular scent at the time of seasonal hormonal changes. The scent message attached to the faeces therefore has nothing to do with sexual signalling. Instead it seems to be entirely concerned with personal identity – an individual labelling or 'calling card' system. In human society we identify people by photographs of their faces, or if they are criminals by their fingerprints, or if they are writing to us by their signatures. With dogs the identity is given by this special scent.

When two high-status dogs meet they stand head to tail and sniff one another in the anal region. Their stiffly erect tails, quivering slightly, have the effect of squeezing the anal glands tight and exuding a small quantity of their strong-smelling contents. Both dogs are fascinated by these odours, which they read with their noses in the same way we read friends' faces with our eyes when we greet them. Just how much detail is carried by this scent – whether it tells about mood, health, and so on – is not yet known, but it is clearly of great importance in the social lives of dogs. This is why, if these glands become blocked, it is such a social disaster for their owners. And this is why any dog suffering in this way puts such earnest effort into dragging the offending organs along the ground, trying to free them of their blockage.

XXVII

HOW DOES A BITCH DEAL WITH HER NEW-BORN PUPPIES?

THE BITCH'S PREGNANCY LASTS NINE WEEKS. THE DAY before giving birth she becomes restless and goes off her food. She grows more aggressive towards strangers but more friendly towards her human 'family'. If some kind of whelping box has been provided for her, she retires to it just before the birth of the litter and lies in it, on her side, with her back to the wall and her head facing the entrance. Rapid breathing alternates with slow breathing as the first birth becomes imminent. As the pup is born her body may shiver and her hind legs twitch slightly. The pups appear at intervals of roughly half an hour, and after each one she goes through a set routine of removing the birth sac, licking the pup's body until it starts breathing, biting through the umbilical cord at a point about two to three inches from the pup's belly, eating the afterbirth and then nudging the puppy towards her body. After this she rests, curled around the puppy, and awaits the next arrival. The typical litter of five pups takes several hours to deliver.

In all these respects the birth of the young and the behaviour of the mother are the same as in the case of the cat. There is, however, an interesting difference connected with the preparation of the bed on which the mother gives birth. The bitch makes frantic digging movements on the floor of the whelping box, but no such actions are observed on the part of the pregnant cat. This reflects a key difference in the behaviour of the wild counterparts of domestic dogs and cats. Cats may dig in the earth when they are burying their faeces, but they do not employ burrowing or tunnelling actions when preparing their breeding dens. The wild cat searches and searches until it finds a suitable, ready-made cavity (which is why domestic cats spend so much time exploring dark cupboards all over the house), but the wolf digs its own home in the earth. And an impressive home it is. Usually located on a hillside near water, where there is good drainage but also a convenient drinking supply, the entrance to the den is often under a rock or a tree-trunk which provides protection from cave-ins. The entrance itself is about two feet wide and leads to a huge tunnel up to fourteen feet in length, at the end of which there is an enlarged cavity, where the young are born and spend the first three weeks of their lives. Some wolf dens have several entrances and all are constructed with a great deal of energetic digging and earth-removal. What is more, the she-wolf is not satisfied with a single den. In case of disturbance she builds a second one nearby to which she can carry the young in an emergency.

All this is a far cry from a domestic dog trying to dig a hole in the floor of its whelping box, but it is important to remember the role of the human house in the dog's mind.

The typical house has several doors which lead through passages into rooms. In dog terms this means that the whole house is a huge den with various entrances leading through tunnels into enlarged cavities. In other words, the humans have already done the 'digging' for the pregnant bitch. All that is missing is the gently curved floor of the whelping cavity itself. This the bitch attempts to rectify with the one remnant of den-making that she still displays – the frantic scratching at the bottom of the box.

When all the puppies have been safely delivered, cleaned, and have nuzzled up to her reclining body, the bitch rests and the litter starts to feed, guzzling the first-milk, or *colostrum*, so vital in providing them with immunity against disease. Another difference between dogs and cats soon emerges, for puppies do not seem to have the same degree of 'nipple ownership' that is found in kittens. With kittens, each individual develops its own personal food station, but with puppies it remains a system of 'feed anywhere'. The reason for the difference no doubt lies in the fact that kittens have sharp claws and puppies do not. Squabbling between kittens would be more painful for the mother, and nipple ownership avoids this. For the bitch, with her blunt-clawed offspring, an occasional scrabbling for position causes no problems.

AT WHAT RATE DO PUPPIES DEVELOP?

THE PUPPIES, BORN BLIND AND DEAF, VARY QUITE considerably in size and weight, according to the breed of the mother. A wolf-cub weighs about one pound at birth.

The average litter size is five. For those who like accurate figures, an analysis of 506 litters gave a precise average figure of 4.92. Litters of more than twenty puppies have been recorded in rare and exceptional cases.

During the first days of life the puppy spends 90 per cent of its time sleeping and the other 10 per cent at the nipple. This is the drowsy 'neonatal phase'.

At thirteen days, the eyes open, but, as with many of these figures, there is considerable breed variation. For example, at this stage nine out of ten Fox Terrier puppies have opened their eyes, but only one out of ten Beagles have done so. It is not until the age of twenty-one days that all pups of all breeds can see. The ears become active at about twenty days, with the first 'startle response'.

When they are three weeks old, the first signs of tail-wagging and barking appear, and the puppies make special trips away from the nest to urinate and defecate.

By the time they are four weeks old, the puppies should weigh roughly seven times their birth-weight, if they are developing normally. They are now entering the 'socialization phase' during which their main preoccupation becomes playing and learning to be a member of a highly social species.

At five weeks, the facial muscles are fully developed, giving this new social being its valuable repertoire of visual signals. At six weeks, there is already some immature pack organization, with unfortunate litter runts suffering from gang attacks by their stronger brothers and sisters. At seven weeks, the bitch's milk starts to dry up. This is the best age for a puppy to be sold or given away if it is to adjust well to life in a new home. Again, however, there are some breed differences here, with up to ten weeks preferred in some cases.

The socialization phase comes to an end at about twelve weeks and is followed by the 'juvenile phase'. The puppy is now fully developed socially and in the wild state would start to explore seriously and take part in hunting activities. At sixteen weeks, the permanent teeth begin to erupt and all are through by twenty-four weeks.

At six months male dogs begin to cock their legs when urinating and become sexually mature. Full sexual maturity is usually reached between six and nine months of age in both males and females, with slight variations from breed to breed. Some individuals are late maturers, not becoming completely adult until they are between ten and twelve months old.

HOW ARE THE PUPPIES WEANED?

DURING THE FIRST THREE WEEKS OF LIFE THE PUPPIES gain all their nourishment from their mother's milk. She lies down to suckle them and they stimulate her milk-flow by pressing on her belly with their front paws and sucking on her nipples. She spends nearly all her time with them. Then, when they are between three and four weeks old, she starts to leave them alone for longer periods, and when she returns she is increasingly reluctant to lie down in the nursing posture. The pups, more active now, try to reach her teats and, if they succeed, she permits them to feed from her while she remains standing. As the days pass she becomes increasingly impatient with them and often starts walking away while they try to hang on to her teats and continue suckling. By the time they are five weeks old she may growl at them when they approach her teats, and may even snap at their faces. When she does this she is, however, always careful not to make contact with them. The snapping is merely a deterrent, but it has a startling effect on the young, who are shocked to find their milk supply denied them. During the next two weeks the young may manage to persuade her to provide an occasional feed, but her milk supply is now coming to an end, and by the time they are seven weeks old she is likely to have stopped lactating altogether. At this stage the pups are fully weaned

(although there is some variation, with a few bitches continuing to provide milk for up to ten weeks).

During this gradual withdrawal of the milk supply, dog-breeders are, of course, offering the puppies dishes of milk to lap and special puppy foods. This is extremely convenient for the bitch, who readily accepts their aid. But how do feral dogs, living rough, manage when there are no human owners to assist in the weaning process? The answer is that, under more natural conditions, dogs have a very special method of positive weaning which balances the negative weaning of milk-withdrawal. They offer predigested food to their puppies by a process of regurgitation. In the wild, when the mother starts to leave the litter alone for longer periods, at the age of three to four weeks, she spends her time away from the den hunting. After the kill she eats the food and then returns to the litter. On arrival, her mouth smells of food and this stimulates the young to sniff at her head.

They then begin to lick her mouth, nuzzle her face, nip at her jaws and even paw at her head. In fact, they behave rather like nestling birds and with the same result. Their actions produce an automatic response in the female. No matter how hungry she may be herself, she cannot help reacting to the 'begging' of her pups by disgorging her half-digested kill.

This maternal act of regurgitation provides the litter with the perfect puppy food, bearing in mind that their first teeth are only just beginning to break through and they are as yet unable to chew properly. During the weeks that follow, as her milk supply dries up, she provides more and more solid food for the growing pups, until this becomes their only source of nutrition. By the time they are twelve weeks old they will have begun to hunt for themselves, although they can still expect a little parental help.

Domesticated bitches, rearing litters under human supervision, frequently fail to show this regurgitation behaviour. The puppies going through the weaning process are so well fed by their human owners that they fail to trigger off the disgorging reaction. Even so, the ancient response does occasionally occur. Some naive owners are upset by this and telephone their vet in panic, reporting that their nursing bitch is starting to vomit and must be ill. Misguidedly they mop up the regurgitated food to prevent the pups from touching it, in case it is infected, thus robbing the litter of its most natural weaning diet.

Observation of wolves breeding in the wild reveals that food-disgorging plays an even larger role in the social life of the dog's original ancestor. When the she-wolf goes to earth to produce her litter, she herself is fed regurgitated food by the rest of the pack. Confined to the den during the crucial first days of the litter's life, she is fed repeatedly in this way. Then, when the cubs are being weaned, she sets off hunting herself to bring them her special predigested offerings. But she is not alone in this. Other pack members – even males – do the same. Indeed, the male wolves are amazingly attentive to the cubs, making trips of up to twenty miles to find prey and then hastening home to present the food to the young before the process of digestion has gone too far.

There are two interesting refinements in this wolf behaviour. The adults themselves are often prepared to eat stale or even putrid meat, but they never offer such items to their cubs. The litter, with their more delicate stomachs, are given only freshly killed meat. Also, the amount given is carefully rationed out, with the adults disgorging small, separate piles of food, thus ensuring that each cub can enjoy an undisturbed feed.

Later, when the cubs have developed a good set of sharp teeth, the adults switch to carrying home large hunks of meat in their mouths, instead of swallowing it first and predigesting it. This often involves great feats of strength, one wolf mother, for example, bringing her litter half a moose's leg, which she had carried in her jaws for over a mile.

If domestic dogs seem rather insipid parents compared with their wild ancestors, it must be remembered that, to dogs, their human owners are simply other 'pack members', so when these helpful companions offer puppy food to the litter it is a perfectly natural act of co-operation. Members of the wolf-pack would do just the same for any litter. The pressure on the domestic bitch is therefore removed and she accepts the human aid without question.

There is one final aspect of weaning that deserves a brief mention. If we find the idea of regurgitated food mildly disgusting, it is worth remembering that, before the invention of baby foods, human mothers weaned their offspring in a very similar manner. Mothers in primitive tribal societies chewed food up into a soft paste and then transferred it, mouth-to-mouth, to their babies. It was, incidentally, this weaning action which gave rise to the human act of exchanging loving kisses. So when a dog licks his owner's face, the comment 'he's kissing me' is closer to the truth than most people realize.

WHY DO PUPPIES CHEW SLIPPERS?

MANY OWNERS FIND THAT OLDER PUPPIES GO through a phase when they become particularly destructive. Favourite targets are slippers and gloves, but children's toys, newspapers, magazines and even the morning mail on the doormat may suffer. Apart from gnawing and chewing these objects, the puppies can also be seen shaking them vigorously, as though trying to kill them. Papers may be torn completely to shreds, as if they are dead birds that need to be plucked of their troublesome feathers. And some owners have noted with exasperation that if the post is attacked, it is always the interesting letters that are savaged, while the bills are left irritatingly intact. (This last point is not a joke. Bills usually come in brown envelopes which are less conspicuous to a dog than white ones.)

Several features of puppyhood are significant here. First, there is simple playfulness. Growing pups are programmed to explore everything in their environment. Dogs are opportunists in the wild and must develop a broad knowledge of the properties of every object in their world. The domestic animal may have a more secure existence, but it has lost very little of its ancestral behaviour.

Second, there is the problem of teething. The adult dentition is acquired between the ages of four and six months and at this time there is an increased need to chew on tough objects, to help the new teeth break through. Soft, commercial dog-food is useless in this respect, and unless the dog is given suitably hard food objects to chew on, it will seek other, less acceptable items for this action.

Third, there is the 'pre-hunting' phase of a growing puppy's life, when it is large enough to be interested in prey, but not yet very efficient at catching it. During this time, when well-nourished growth is so important, adults (in a wild context) bring hunks of meat back to the home base for the youngsters. So the stage of 'older puppyhood' is characterized as a time when big dogs (= human owners) leave things lying around on the ground for small dogs to eat. It is therefore perfectly natural, and in no way perverse, for a young dog to look upon a slipper on the carpet or a package on the doormat as a welcome gift from the senior members of the group. To be scolded for chewing up such objects must be both puzzling and hurtful for an eager puppy doing its best to adjust to living in a human 'pack'.

XXXI

HOW DO DOGS
PERFORM THEIR COURTSHIP?

THERE IS A SPECIAL FORM OF SEXUAL INEQUALITY among dogs. In humans, both male and female are sexually active all through the year. In many other animals, both male and female come into breeding condition together for a brief period of intense sexual activity. But with dogs, the male is sexually ready all through the year, while the female has only two limited periods of heat. This means that the unfortunate male dogs spend most of the year in a state of sexual frustration.

That is not all. When the long-awaited period of female heat does arrive, the bitch spends the first phase of it living up to her name. In fact, there will only be a few days in the early spring, and again in the autumn, when she will accept the male's advances. So, for the lucky male domestic dog, which has not been castrated by his owners, has not been brought forcibly to heel at every sight of a bitch, and has not been kept shut in when a bitch is on heat in the neighbourhood, which has not been attacked and driven off by rival dogs, and has not been rejected by the typically choosy bitch ... there will be only fifty out of fifty-two weeks of sexual frustration during the year. For the rest there will be fifty-two weeks out of fifty-two.

Females also suffer. If they have not been spayed, their brief heats may see them shut indoors, doused with anti-sexual chemicals, or forced to wear the canine equivalent of chastity belts. The fortunate ones, taken to a stud dog for mating, frequently have their amours reduced to the equivalent of a 'short time' in a red light district.

The owners cannot be blamed, of course. If canine sexuality were allowed to take its course, the whole world would be awash with puppies. As it is, the many dogs' homes have to kill thousands of surplus animals every year. But this does mean that the details of canine courtship are less commonly observed than they might be. In the rare event of males and females being allowed full licence to express themselves sexually, this is what happens:

In the first stage of heat, called the pro-oestrous (which means literally the pre-frenzy), the bitch starts to become restless and to wander more and more. She drinks much more than usual and urinates a great deal as she wanders. The fragrance of this urine makes a great impression on the males. They sniff it eagerly, then raise their heads and gaze into the distance in silent concentration, like professional wine-tasters savouring a rare vintage. Strongly aroused by this chemical signal, they start to seek out the female, responding especially to the odour of her vaginal secretions, which they can detect from a great distance. These secretions are caused by a discharge from her increasingly swollen genitals. This discharge becomes bloody towards the end of the pro-oestrous period and some people have

referred to it as the bitch 'menstruating', for obvious reasons. This is incorrect, however. Menstruation is caused by the breakdown of the lining of the uterus following an unsuccessful ovulation. The bleeding in the core of the bitch occurs before ovulation and is caused by changes in the walls of the vagina in preparation for copulation.

During this pro-oestrous period, which lasts about nine days, the female is so attractive to the male because of her odours that she may be relentlessly pursued by hopeful suitors. Since she is not yet ovulating, she rejects all advances. It is now that she is at her most bitchy. She may attack the amorous male, chase him, growl at him, bite him and generally threaten him. If she is less aggressive, she either runs away, or whirls round the moment he tries to mount her. Another strategy is promptly to sit down the moment he shows excited interest in her rear end.

This may seem like a pointless period of teasing the male. If she will not accept him, why send out all those appealing scent signals? The answer is that it is important for her to ensure that all potential mates are well aware of her condition, so that when the crucial moment comes she will not find herself mateless. Ovulation occurs spontaneously on the second day of the oestrous period proper. A day or two after that the bitch is ready to be fertilized. If males are absent then she will have to wait another six months for her next chance.

The oestrous period itself also lasts for about nine days. The female's discharge becomes clearer and more watery, indicating that the vagina is ready for mating. Now the courtship proper begins. The earlier behaviour of the bitch gives way to a new pattern in which she runs towards the male, then retreats; runs towards him, then retreats. In the unlikely event that he ignores this invitation, she prances all round him, strikes him with her forepaws and may even mount him. Usually, however, he gives chase, and eventually the scampering pair come together and examine one another's bodies. First there is intense nose-to-nose sniffing and perhaps some ear-licking. Then there is mutual nose-to-rump sniffing, with the male playing the major role as he makes a final check on her sexual condition and her scent-appeal. After this he usually comes up to the side of the bitch and rests his chin across her back. If she stands still and does not move away, he then swivels round and mounts her, after which copulation begins.

The female is far from passive in this procedure. If she is at the peak of her heat and the male is one she likes (and she may still be choosy even at this stage), she will do everything she can to help him achieve his goal. After 'standing' for him – that is to say, remaining still as he nuzzles and examines her – she will give him a specific invitation signal to mount. This consists of swinging her tail over to one side, to expose her genitals. If the male reacts by mounting, he may have difficulty in finding his target. He starts making pelvic thrusts on a hit-and-miss basis and, as she feels his error, she carefully moves her rump, up a little, down a little, left a little, until she has skilfully corrected his aim. If, as the male copulates, he takes the scruff of her neck in his jaws (which is not a regular feature but does happen occasionally) she does not object.

In almost all respects this courtship behaviour – if permitted to run its course – is the same as in the dog's wild ancestor, the wolf. Domestication has changed little in the sexual sequence. The amount of courtship has, however, been drastically reduced in relation to copulation, especially in the pedigree world of stud dogs and champion bitches. In one wolf-pack, for example, it was observed that a total of 1,296 courtships led to only thirty-one full copulations. In pedigree matings there may be occasional refusals, but most meetings are so well organized that nearly all encounters lead to a successful conclusion.

The reason for the low chance (2.4 per cent) of a wolf courtship succeeding is that there are much stronger mate preferences in the wild. Males and females may not form lifelong monogamous pairs, but they do have intense sexual likes and dislikes which mean that unlucky suitors perform many a hopeless and ultimately futile courtship display. Whether similar preferences would develop if a group of domestic dogs went wild and formed an independent pack is hard to say, although it seems likely, as so little else seems to have been altered by domestication.

WHY DO THE BITCH AND THE DOG BECOME 'TIED' TOGETHER DURING THE MATING ACT?

O NE OF THE STRANGEST FEATURES OF CANINE sexuality is 'the tie'. After the male has mounted the female and performed some pelvic thrusts, he finds it impossible to withdraw from her. The mated pair appear to be locked together. Even if they struggle to separate themselves they cannot manage to do so. They remain helplessly 'engaged' in this way for some time, looking very vulnerable, before they finally pull apart, lick their genitals and then relax.

For many years canine experts have puzzled over the function of this peculiar element in the breeding behaviour of dogs. Some have frankly admitted that they can see no point in it. Others have guessed wildly, rather than admit defeat. Before considering their explanations, it is worth taking a closer look at precisely what happens when the male mates with the female.

Once the female has signalled to the male to mount her, he clasps her with his front legs and attempts to insert his penis. At this stage the penis is only in a state of semi-erection. He starts to make a few vigorous pelvic thrusts and achieves intromission. While clinging to the female's body with his front legs, he presses his chest and some-times also his chin on to her back. She stands completely still, with her tail kept to one side, facilitating the entry of his penis.

The male now performs a highly characteristic treading movement with his hind legs, rocking his rear end from side to side. These pelvic swayings thrust his penis deeper into the female. At the base of his penis is a swelling called the *bulbus glandis* and once this has entered the female it starts to swell. The whole penis now becomes fully erect. At the same time the female's vagina becomes strongly constricted. Together the male's inflation and the female's compression create the powerful lock or 'tie'. After the tie has taken place there are some more pelvic thrusts and then the male ejaculates.

At this point he usually dismounts quietly by placing his front legs on the ground alongside the female's body. Because their genitals remain locked together, this leaves him in a rather awkward, twisted posture. He corrects it by lifting one of his hind legs over her back. He turns away from her and the pair now stand, tied together, but facing in opposite directions. They may remain quietly together in this fashion for the rest of the tie, or they may start to struggle. The female may decide to walk off, in which case the male will resist and there may be a great deal of yelp-ing and whining. If the pair are disturbed or harassed, they may writhe around and even fall over in their attempts to separate themselves, but the tie nearly always holds firm. Despite the fact that they cause one another considerable pain during these struggles, there is no evidence that any lasting damage is done to their genitals.

Authorities differ in their observations of how long the tie lasts. Five minutes is one of the shortest recorded, but the figure is usually much higher – 15, 20, 25, 30, 36, 45, 75, and even as long as 120 minutes, have been reported in different cases. The most usual period seems to be about twenty to thirty minutes, with the very high figures rather rare. The tie ends when the male's penis starts to lose its full erection and he is at last able to withdraw.

That is the pattern of behaviour and here are some of the past explanations that have been offered: first, there is the theory that the tie helps to strengthen the emotional attachment between the male and female. The idea is that by prolonging the mating act it becomes more personal and assists in the formation of a pair-bond. It is true that the male and female, if permitted, will become closer after mating and experiencing the tie, but it seems highly unlikely that the usually painful process of being locked together helplessly for minutes on end will itself endear the dog and bitch to one another. It is possible but improbable.

Second, it has been proposed that the lock makes mating more comfortable for the male. It seems likely that such a comment could only come from someone used to 'arranged marriages' between experienced stud dogs and pedigree bitches, where the pair are isolated from other dogs and calmed by their owners. Under such circumstances the male and female may simply stand together quietly until the tie is over, giving the impression of resting. In a more natural situation, with feral dogs, park dogs, street dogs, or wolves, the tie is usually far from peaceful and gives the impression of acute discomfort for at least some of the time.

Third is the strange suggestion that the tie is a defensive device that gives the mating pair 'teeth at both ends'

should any other animals try to interfere. Anyone who has observed a tie in a wolf-pack will appreciate that the tied male is in reality extremely vulnerable. There is little co-ordination between his movements and those of the female if a dominant animal comes close.

Fourth, it has been claimed that the tie prevents semen leakage from the female. Why a bitch should be so badly designed as a recipient of male sperm is not explained.

A much more acceptable explanation has emerged recently from artificial insemination experiments, and we now know what is taking place inside the reproductive systems of the mating pair. Instead of a simple, single ejaculate of the kind familiar to humans, the dog goes through three distinct phases. The first phase takes between thirty and fifty seconds. This initial ejaculate is a clear, spermless fluid. During the second phase, timed at fifty to ninety seconds, the ejaculate is thick and white and contains 1,250 million sperm.

The third and final phase consists of a much larger quantity of ejaculate, again a clear, spermless liquid. This is a prostatic fluid which goes on being produced as long as the tie persists. Obviously the function of the prolonged tie is to give the male time to produce this last fluid, which swills into the female's reproductive tract and activates the sperm that have just been deposited there.

So we now know the mystery of the 'tie'. It is not something which follows ejaculation, but something which accompanies it. Because human ejaculation is so brief, we have been misled into thinking that the dog behaves in the same way. The idea of a male dog ejaculating for half an hour seems strange to us. It is certainly hard to understand why the process of canine insemination should be so cumbersome and protracted. But given the fact that it is, the tie makes sense as a foolproof way of buying time to ensure that the delivery of sperm is successful.

114

XXXIII

WHY DO SOME DOGS
TRY TO MATE WITH YOUR LEG?

MANY PEOPLE HAVE EXPERIENCED THE EMBARRASSING moment when their host's male dog has suddenly clasped its front feet around their leg and started making vigorous pelvic thrusts. Why do these dogs embark upon such an unpromising activity? The answer is that dogs pass through a special socialization phase when they are puppies, during which time they establish their identity. This critical period lasts from the age of four to twelve weeks, and any species sharing this time with them in close and friendly proximity becomes *their* species. For all pet dogs there are always two species present during this crucial stage of growing up – dogs and humans. As a result they become 'mental hybrids', powerfully attached to both species. For the rest of their lives they remain at ease in both canine and human society. The members of their human family serve well enough as an adopted 'pack'. Humans share their food, share their den, go out patrolling the territory together, play together, indulge in a little social grooming, perform the required greeting ceremonies and generally act the role of dog companions with alacrity. Dog society and human society make a good match. Only where sex is concerned does the relationship break down.

Fortunately, there are some powerful inborn responses involved in canine sexual attraction, which usually serve to keep dogs aimed in the right direction. Since humans do not possess the dog's particular erotic fragrance, they do not normally trigger the sexual responses of the male dogs that share their homes. As far as the dogs are concerned, people are simply 'members of their pack who are never in sexual condition'.

All should be well but, sadly for most male dogs, encounters with bitches on heat are abnormally rare events in their domesticated lives. A level of sexual frustration builds up where even the family cat begins to look appealing. At this point a randy dog will try to mount almost anything that will stay still long enough, including cats, other male dogs, cushions and human legs. Human legs are attractive because they are easy to clasp. The choice of a leg rather than some more appropriate part of the human anatomy is due simply to the awkward, undog-like shape of human beings. They are too big and too tall, making the leg the only easily accessible region for a last-resort sexual advance. The correct response to a leg-clasping dog is compassion rather than anger. It is we, after all, who have condemned such dogs to an abnormally celibate existence. A polite rejection of their advances is all that is needed, not angry punishment.

The comment about the dog's interest in the family cat was not intended to be facetious. Some sexually frustrated dogs do try to mate with cats, but this only happens when the animals concerned grew up together as puppies and kittens. A close relationship with young cats during the critical phase of puppy development simply adds felines to the category of 'my species' in the canine mind. A puppy that has played with (a) other puppies in its litter, (b) the family kitten, and (c) its human owners, during the socialization phase of four to twelve weeks, will have a triple attachment that will last a lifetime.

There is another side of the coin to this attachment process. The *absence* of a species during the socialization period in the puppy's development will mean that it is automatically something to be avoided later on. This applies even to the puppy's own true species. If a tiny pup is taken away from its mother before its eyes and ears are open – say, when it is only a week old – and hand-reared in isolation, it will become massively attached to humans but will always be shy with other dogs in later life. It is therefore a mistake to remove a puppy from its family too soon. If there is a disaster, with the mother dying and only one puppy surviving, for example, then it is important to try and have other puppies or dogs around the young one as it is being hand-reared, so that it becomes used to the company of its own kind during its critical growth period.

If a puppy is left in the company of its own canine family but kept completely away from humans until it is past the age of twelve weeks, it will never become tame and friendly with people in later life. Puppies reared in a field on an experimental farm, where they had no close contact with people until the litter was fourteen weeks old, were effectively like wild animals. The idea that the domestic dog is in some way a 'genetically tame' animal is therefore not true. The suggestion that wolves are more 'savage' and untameable than dogs is also incorrect. A wolf-cub taken at a young enough stage of development becomes a remarkably friendly companion, so much so that most people, seeing one being taken for a walk on a collar and lead, would imagine that it was just another large dog. Indeed, on one occasion a tame adult wolf was taken from England to the United States on the *Queen Elizabeth*, registered as an Alsatian, without causing any comment. It was given a daily walk around the deck and was cheerfully petted by passengers and crew, who would have been horrified had they known its true identity.

WHY DO DOGS TRY TO SLEEP ON THEIR OWNERS' BEDS?

MANY AN OWNER HAS SUFFERED FROM A PET DOG demanding to be allowed to sleep on the bed. Toy dogs sometimes win this battle, but if a Great Dane succeeds it may end up as the subject of a custody dispute in a divorce court. Why are they so keen to pass the night so close to their owners?

The answer is that, in many ways, they never develop past the puppy stage. Because, even as adults, they look upon their human owners as pseudo-parents, it is perfectly natural for them to want to curl up next to their 'mother's' body. In this context, 'mother' is not necessarily the woman. If the dog is more closely attached to the man of the house, it is he who will become the surrogate mother and will be the desired object for contact-sleeping. Either way, it can put a considerable strain on marital relations and has in some cases, both literally and legally, led to the splitting-up of a married couple.

Even if, by strict training, the family dog is kept off the bed, it will still want to sleep as close as possible to its 'pack'. In the wild state, after they have left the nest, young wolves prefer to sleep reasonably close to one another. Only a beaten pack-outcast would be found sleeping at a distance from the group. It follows that a dog that is shut right away from its human owners at night must also feel like an outcast from its adopted pack. Where there is a group of guard-dogs or a pack of hounds this presents no problems, of course, because the animals have one another's company. But where there is a solitary pet dog living with a family, it will find it hard to understand why it is being shunned at bedtime and kept forcibly away from its human companions. In the end most families work out their own compromise, with the dog being allowed as close to the bedroom as possible without becoming a bed-time nuisance.

WHY ARE SOME DOGS
DIFFICULT TO CONTROL?

MOST DOMESTIC DOGS FIT INTO HUMAN FAMILY LIFE extremely well, but occasionally a male dog becomes a trouble-maker. He bites visitors without provocation, urinates in the house and stubbornly refuses to obey orders. On a family outing it is he who takes his owner for a walk rather than the other way around. He stops when he feels like it and moves on when the mood takes him. All attempts to tug him along on his lead are vigorously resisted. At feeding times he may ignore his food bowl and have to be tempted with special titbits. How does a pet dog develop this type of personality?

The answer is painfully obvious, although the owners of such dogs are always reluctant to accept it. The fact is that male dogs of this kind have simply been allowed to become the dominant members of their 'pack'. Each male wolf tries to achieve this status in a wild pack, and domestic dogs are no different in this respect. Humans have a great advantage over their dogs in the dominance stakes, because they are physically larger, but if the animals are unduly pampered they will make a bid for pack leadership. If they win one confrontation after another they eventually arrive at the conclusion that they are indeed now the dominant members of the group.

This need not involve actual fights with their owners. A confrontation can be won simply because the dog manages to overrule his human companions when they wish to do one thing and he insists on doing something else. After a long string of such 'wins', the dog considers he is dominant and then starts to behave accordingly. This includes urinating inside the house to show that it is *his* territory, and making all decisions about 'what happens next' when out for a walk. This is not abnormal behaviour. It is perfectly natural for a dominant animal to take the lead when the 'pack' is out 'hunting'. So he finds it hard to understand why his decisions about starting and stopping should be challenged. What's more, one of his leadership duties is defending his subordinates (that is, his human companions) against attack from strangers. Hence his assaults on postmen, milkmen and other visitors arriving at the door.

Some dog-trainers are able to cure these difficult dogs by a course of disciplinary training, so that they are bullied into being subordinate pack members again, but there is a danger in too much of this kind of treatment. The outcome of undue emphasis on discipline and obedience is the production of a fawning, characterless dog of an unattractively submissive kind. The secret where dogs are concerned is to aim at a happy medium – to balance ultimate control with as much freedom as possible.

XXXVI

WHY DO DOGS HAVE DEW-CLAWS?

DEW-CLAWS ARE THE REMNANTS OF THE FIRST TOES of the remote ancestors of the dog. When the members of the dog family began to specialize as runners, during the course of evolution, their legs became longer and their feet narrowed from five toes to four. The first toes vanished altogether from the hind legs of wild dogs, but those on the front legs survived as vestiges which no longer touched the ground.

This design gives wolves an impressive turn of speed, 35-40 m.p.h. having been recorded on several occasions over distances of up to a quarter of a mile. Single bounds of sixteen feet have been measured. Endurance over long distances is also remarkable. Huskies, the breed closest to the wolf ancestor, have been known to draw a sledge for over 500 miles in a total time of only eighty hours.

Becoming specialized in running meant sacrifices in other directions. The ability of dogs to climb and jump worsened as their running improved. But their increased speed and greater stamina on the chase became immensely efficient and successful enough to enable the wild dogs to survive worldwide, from the hot tropics to the frozen wastelands.

So dew-claws should be on their way out, a casualty of the coming-of-age of canines as track athletes. But if this is so, then it seems strange that many breeds of domestic dogs appear to be reversing the trend. One would imagine that modern dogs, being even further removed from the ancient canine ancestor than are wolves or Dingoes, would have lost all their dew-claws, the 'thumbs' of the front feet following the 'big toes' of the hind feet into oblivion. Instead the reverse is the case. Many breeds of modern dogs have all four dew-claws present. The hind ones are never as solid or as well attached as the front ones, usually consisting of no more than a free bone and a claw loosely connected to the foot by a small flap of skin, but even so they represent a slight turnabout in dog evolution. Breeds with these hind-foot dew-claws, however vestigial they may be, are closer in that respect at least to the ancient canine ancestor than either the Dingo or the wolf. Why has this return towards a primeval condition taken place?

The answer lies in the process known as *neoteny* – the survival of infantile characteristics in adult animals. This is what has happened to dogs during the 10,000 years of their controlled breeding by man. They have, in effect, become juvenile wolves. They can breed, but they retain many of their young behaviour patterns, such as playfulness and obedience to a pseudo-parent – the human owner. They also retain a number of juvenile anatomical features, such as the floppy ears seen in so many breeds today.

Retaining the extra dew-claws is part of this process. We may have bred a number of increasingly extreme features into the different modern breeds, but in other ways they are more primitive than the highly specialized wolf from which they were all derived. In other words, when we set about converting the wolf into the dog we turned the clock backwards as well as forwards.

It is interesting that dog-breeders intuitively feel that there is something wrong with dew-claws and advise that they should be removed when puppies are three to six days old. They recognize it as an 'unspecializing trend' and correct it. The excuse is given that if these vestigial claws are allowed to remain, they may become caught in under-growth and torn. Bearing in mind that they are on the insides of the legs and above ground, this is a fairly unlikely accident and a trivial excuse, but the unconscious urge to 'refine' the dog's legs is strong enough to overlook this. (Except in certain specific breeds, such as the Briard and the Pyrenean Mountain Dog, where hind-leg dew-claws have to be retained to comply with breed standards.)

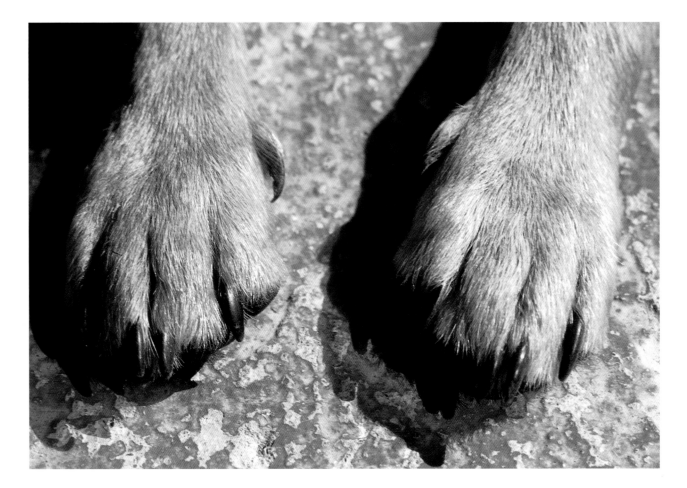

XXXVII

WHY DO SOME DOGS
CHASE THEIR OWN TAILS?

EVERY SO OFTEN A DOG CAN BE SEEN CIRCLING ROUND and round at high speed, chasing its own tail. It snaps its jaws at the vanishing tail, then spins round in hot pursuit, sometimes circling so many times that it becomes dizzy and disoriented. For the human observer, what starts out as an amusing folly on the part of the dog and seems to be no more than a simple play pattern, eventually becomes disturbing. It begins to look like a stereotype that has become a behavioural abnormality, rather than a rhythmic game. Sadly, this is not too far from the truth, because persistent tail-chasing is usually the failing of dogs that have been kept in unnaturally boring conditions.

Dogs are social beings and they are also intensely exploratory. If they are deprived of companions – both canine and human – or if they are kept in a constrained or monotonous environment, they suffer. The worst mental punishment a dog can be given is to be kept alone in a tightly confined space where nothing varies. Fortunately this rarely happens with domestic dogs. But wild dogs in zoos have often been housed in small, cramped, empty cages, condemned to a life sentence of solitary confinement. Observation of such animals has revealed that they frequently develop 'tics' and stereotyped actions, such as paw-biting, tail-chewing, neck-twisting, pacing and other damaging patterns of repetitive behaviour. Sometimes these tics become so savage that dogs repeatedly bite right into their flesh and develop running sores. This self-punishment may seem destructive, but it has the effect of providing acute stimulation in a world that has become an unbearable limbo of boredom. Tail-chasing is a mild form of this type of behaviour. It is often seen in a puppy that has recently been isolated from its litter-mates. Taken to a new home, it is suddenly robbed of all the rough-and-tumble play so typical of a lively litter, and it must seek new forms of stimulation. If its owners do not play with it enough, the puppy may find it difficult to start up a 'game' and it is then that the tail becomes the best 'companion' available. There is no harm in this, providing the circling does not become a compulsive obsession. Many lonely puppies do it for a while and then grow out of the habit. Only when it persists into adulthood does it indicate a fault in the dog's environment, and a greater need for social interaction and adventure. It can usually be cured simply by increasing these aspects of the animal's life.

The only exception to this rule is when a dog is suffering from some stubborn irritation in the tail region, such as swollen anal glands or lasting pain from a badly docked tail. But in such cases other, more specific responses, such as rump-dragging and tail-nibbling, are more likely to occur.

XXXVIII

WHY ARE SOME BREEDS OF DOG SO SMALL?

WHATEVER THEIR ORIGINS, SMALL BREEDS OF DOG remain popular today because they make ideal child substitutes. Bigger dogs make perfect companions on long walks and satisfyingly act out the role of obedient subordinates when they 'stay', 'sit' and 'fetch', but they lack important infantile qualities. In their playfulness and friendliness they may be juvenile, but they are not babyish. To arouse maternal feelings in their owners, dogs must transmit a special set of signals and this is where the smaller breeds come into their own.

To understand this it is necessary to look at the infantile properties of the human baby that have particular appeal for its loving parents. To start with, it only weighs a fraction of the adult – about seven pounds at birth, fourteen at five months and twenty-one at twelve months. This, and its small size, make it easy to pick up, carry and cuddle. Its body is more rounded and less angular than that of human adults and it is softer to touch. Its face is flatter and its eyes proportionally bigger. It has a high-pitched voice.

Turning from human babies to small dogs, it is clear that they all satisfy some of these criteria of infant-appeal and that certain breeds, such as the Pekinese, satisfy all of them. As regards body weight, they fall into three groups. Giving approximate figures, they are as follows:

1   Dogs with the weight of a new-born human infant: Chihuahua (4 lb), Maltese Terrier (5 lb), Pomeranian (6 lb), Yorkshire Terrier (7 lb) and Griffon (9 lb).

2   Dogs with the weight of a five-month-old infant: Pekinese (12 lb), Shih Tzu (14 lb), King Charles's Spaniel (15 lb), and Pug (16 lb).

3   Dogs with the weight of a one-year-old human infant: Dachshund (21 lb) and Corgi (22 lb).

Such dogs are the ideal weight for a 'parental' human being to pick up and carry. Many of these breeds are rounder and softer than the larger breeds of dog, making them the perfect object to pet and cuddle. Nearly all of them have flatter faces than big dogs, and some have been subjected to selective breeding to produce extremes of flatness that approximate to the profile of the human baby. The Griffon, the Pug and the Pekinese fall into this category. And several of them have the huge, bulging eyes so typical of the human new-born. All of them, because of their small body size, have much higher pitched voices than the larger breeds.

Put together this means that the smaller dog breeds (of which only a cross-section has been mentioned here) cannot help transmitting powerful infantile signals to their owners, whose inborn parental responses are automatically triggered, making them more loving, protective and emotionally attached to their particular pets. This is in no way a criticism of such relationships. Some authorities have frowned on the lavishing of so much love on members of another species. They feel that human parental care should be directed exclusively towards human infants and not 'wasted' elsewhere. Curiously, the people who hold such views are not usually very good parents themselves. It is probably their guilt that makes them feel as they do. People who do lavish attention on small dogs are generally those who have been such good parents towards their human children that they have a positive surplus of parental love which they wish to continue to express, or those who, for whatever reason, have no children of their

own. In all such instances the relationship between human owner and small dog has the potential to be mutually extremely fulfilling.

Some of the smaller breeds seem to have started out as companion dogs, but others gained their diminutive proportions for different reasons. Terriers, for instance, as their name implies, are 'earth-dogs', bred originally as diggers-out of vermin. Small bodies were essential for this purpose and the ideal terrier was said to be a dog that would 'enter the earth with much fury'. But then, having been bred for this industrious and hard-working purpose, the Terriers were taken up as show dogs and pets and soon found their shrunken size a great advantage in other, less demanding directions.

WHY DO SOME BREEDS OF DOG HAVE SUCH SHORT LEGS?

THERE ARE TWO DISTINCT PRESSURES AT WORK HERE. One is the practical need for dogs with legs short enough for the animals to be sent down burrows after underground prey. The Dachshund is a classic example of this type. The name means literally 'badger-dog', the breed having been developed in Germany to pursue badgers into their burrows and attack them there. Various kinds of Terriers have also had their legs genetically shortened by selective breeding, with similar tunnelling duties in mind. Other breeds, such as the oriental Pekinese, have had their leg-length reduced as part of the process of 'baby-making'. Because of their pet function of acting as child substitutes, they are not only made smaller, but are also given legs short enough to endow them with the appealing clumsiness of a mobile infant. They cannot bound gracefully over the earth, but must waddle along with the serious concentration of a toddler trying to cope with the mysterious business of getting from A to B.

Because of the less athletic appeal of the short-legged toy dogs, it follows that any short-legged breed, even if originally developed as a burrower, will have its own special attraction as a pet dog. For this reason, many of the Terrier breeds have become immensely popular in a non-working role, as have Dachshunds.

Despite their genetic disability, in terms of fast running and chasing, they have retained the same fighting spirit and enthusiasm for life of any of the big dogs. Their bodies may have been cut short, but they are not short on energy or determination. For pet owners it is this combination of big-dog personality with low-slung, short-stride physical handicap that gives these breeds their special, plucky appeal.

WHY DO SO MANY BREEDS OF DOG
HAVE FLOPPY EARS?

FLOPPY EARS ARE ONLY PRESENT IN WILD DOGS WHEN they are very young. In domestic dogs they are therefore a juvenile characteristic which has been retained into adult life. This is just one more way in which the dog confirms itself as an 'infantilized wolf'. But many domestic dogs do have wolflike, pricked ears, so it is clear that hanging ears are not an inevitable feature of the domestication process. Why then have they been retained – and indeed actively encouraged – in so many different kinds of breeds?

There appear to be three answers to this question. First, an obvious outcome of owning floppy ears is that directional sound detection is impaired. When a prick-eared dog is listening to distant noises it twists and turns its large, erect ears to pin-point the tiniest rustle or murmur. Flop-eared dogs may still be able to hear extremely well, but their detection of the precise direction of a small sound can never be as good. It is claimed that this weakness was deliberately developed in various breeds of hunting dogs that were supposed to be working purely by sight or smell,

and which it was feared might be distracted by irrelevant sounds in the distance. The floppiest ears of all do, of course, belong to that scent-trailing expert – the Bloodhound.

A second attraction of flop-ears is the more submissive look they give to the dogs in question. Most people are aware that an angry dog has pricked ears, fiercely erect, and that a subordinate dog keeps its ears flat against its head as a sign of its low social status. Even if this difference in ear posture has not been consciously analysed, there is nevertheless an undefined feeling that somehow a floppy-eared dog is less savage than a prick-eared one. Finally, there is the anthropomorphic advantage. Humans do not have pricked ears that stick up above the top of the head, but they do often have long hair that flops down on either side of it. This means that very long, drooping ears look superficially like the hanging locks of human hairstyles. Silky-haired breeds such as the Afghan Hound, where the individual hairs are also long and soft, appear even more humanoid and therefore attractive to their owners.

XLI

WHY DO SOME BREEDS OF
DOG HAVE THEIR TAILS DOCKED?

THE FACT THAT MANY DOG-BREEDERS STILL INSIST ON docking the tails of their pedigree puppies, despite mounting hostility from an increasingly wide spectrum of critics, requires some explanation. Who started this strange practice and why was this particular form of mutilation thought necessary or desirable?

First of all, what exactly is docking? It is the surgical removal of all or part of a dog's tail, usually performed with a sharp pair of scissors when a puppy is four days old. The skin of the tail is firmly held just above the point where the tail is to be severed and is tugged up towards the puppy's body so that, when the amputation has been made, there is a slight surplus of skin to fall back and close over the tip of the stump. This reduces bleeding and hastens healing. The bitch is removed from the vicinity of the operation so that she cannot hear the screams of her puppies. After the tails have been cut off, the puppies are returned to their mother and in most cases she licks the tail-stumps and then settles down to suckling the litter again. In rare instances puppies die of shock or excessive bleeding, but most survive and are soon busily feeding from the nipple.

It has been estimated that in Britain about 50,000 pups have been docked each year in recent times, despite the opposition of: the RSPCA, who have been campaigning to have the operation made illegal; the Council of the Royal College of Veterinary Surgeons, who describe docking as 'an unjustified mutilation'; the Council of Europe, who now insist on the prohibition of 'non-curative' operations on dogs; and the British Government, who support the stand taken by the Council of Europe. More than forty breeds are involved, from the huge Old English Sheepdog down to the tiny Yorkshire Terrier.

The reason given by dog-breeders for continuing their 'barbarous custom', as docking was called as long ago as 1802, is that the Show Standards of the dogs in question demand docked tails and that without this special feature their puppies would never stand a chance of becoming valuable champions. Under renewed pressure to alter this state of affairs, a Kennel Club official recently stated publicly that docking should be considered voluntary and that no dog should be penalized in any contest for having a complete tail, regardless of the traditional Show Standards. So the usual reasons of fashion, beauty and breed configuration can no longer find official support even from the Show Dog authority itself, leaving the unrepentant pro-docking lobby somewhat stranded. In desperation they have sought other arguments in favour of a dog having a docked tail. During a public debate two breeders put forward the view that docking prevented their dogs from damaging their tails if they fought later in life. This is like

arguing that if you cut off a man's feet you are protecting him from stubbing his big toe.

Another point put forward in all seriousness is that working dogs may tear their tails when moving through the undergrowth. A veterinary surgeon has described this excuse as 'fatuous rubbish', but despite his enlightened comment this type of claim has a long history. In the past, when dogs were more likely to have to earn their keep, it was generally held that working dogs did benefit from having only a short stump of a tail. Terriers, the most widely docked group, were said to be spared the horror of having rats bite their tails when they went into action as pest-controllers. This too was a fantasy, but one which went unquestioned for many years.

Because working dogs were at one time exempt from a tax levied on sporting dogs, some unfortunate animals were docked simply as a tax avoidance device. Back in the days when this was widespread, most country villages had their own 'tail docker' who, for a small fee, would bite off a puppy's tail with his teeth.

It is hard to grasp how anyone could, in the very first instance, have conceived the eccentric idea of amputating a dog's tail. How did it originate? Most writings on the subject report that its true origin is 'lost in the mists of antiq-uity'. Fortunately, for once, this is not the case. Scholars searching for the oldest dog book in the world discovered that it was written by a Roman agriculturalist called Columella, who was active in the middle of the first century AD. He instructed that forty-day-old puppies should have their tails bitten off and their tail sinews pulled out in order to protect them from rabies. This extraordinary precaution was based on the misconception that rabies was caused by worms inside the dog's body. If a dog's tail is bitten into and pulled off, the tendons of the tail muscles stick out, looking like a cluster of gleaming white worms. It was these sinister-looking tendons that were to cause the loss of literally millions of puppy-dog tails in the centuries that followed. As time passed, new reasons came to replace the original one, but by that stage the act of tail removal had already become entrenched as an accepted part of canine management. Like so many traditions, it was strong enough to outlive its original purpose.

The disadvantage of docking is obvious. It severely damages the important canine tail-wagging system, so vital to dogs' social encounters. Add to this the cruelty of the operation, and there is little wonder that such strenuous steps have been taken to outlaw this superstitious practice that lingers on from the distant days of ancient Rome.

XLII

WHY DO DOGS DISLIKE
SOME STRANGERS MORE THAN OTHERS?

DOGS ARE NEARLY ALWAYS SUSPICIOUS OF STRANGERS who enter their owners' homes and they greet them with a great deal of barking and sniffing. Some visitors have the knack of quickly calming them, while others seem unable to do so and may even be nipped or bitten. What is the difference between them?

The answer lies mostly in the style of the visitors' body movements. Some people have naturally smooth movements, their actions possessing a generally soft and flowing quality. Others are, by nature, rather tense and jerky. They tend to make quick, hesitant movements and these are much more likely to arouse the aggression of the dogs, because they are actions of the kind found in hostile or nervous canine encounters.

If the jumpy, twitchy person also fears dogs, the situation gets worse, because they will start making jerky *retreat* movements and these give signals to the dogs that automatically make them advance and possibly even attack. Pulling away from a barking dog, or performing any kind of rapid withdrawal movement, makes a dog feel suddenly superior and it responds accordingly.

By contrast, the person who 'gets on with dogs' tends to answer greeting with greeting, approaches them rather than withdraws, and offers them some form of gentle hand-contact. This can convert a noisy, barking dog into a fawning tail-wagger in seconds and, after the greeting ceremony is over, the dog will relax and cease to intrude on the newcomer's space. This only works, however, with dogs that are barking, or jumping up while tail-wagging. If, instead, the dog that greets you at someone's front door is stiffly rigid, growling or snarling, and giving you a fixed stare, the only course of action is to stay very still and do nothing – neither advance nor retreat – and hope that the dog's owner will come to your rescue. With such an animal the level of aggression is so high that it is dangerous to give off any signals at all, and complete immobility is the best way to reduce your visual impact on the animal. If you are alone and really worried about the dog's mood, then giving a plaintive puppy whine or whimper might just defuse the situation by arousing the protective parental feelings of the home-defender. But there is no guarantee that this will work, because you are from an 'alien pack' and therefore not to be trusted.

Fortunately, such extreme forms of hostile greeting are rare, unless a dog has been specifically trained to attack intruders. Most dogs simply bark and leap about when a visitor arrives, and they are a push-over for all but the most cynophobic of visitors.

XLIII

DO DOGS HAVE A SIXTH SENSE?

YES, BUT NOT PERHAPS IN THE WAY THAT IS generally envisaged. There is nothing supernatural about canine sensitivities. They can all be explained by biological mechanisms, although it is true that we are only just beginning to understand some of them. For instance, dogs can find their way home from long distances, over terrain with which they are not familiar. This is a quality they share with cats and many other species of animals. It seems to be based on an appreciation of subtle differences and changes in the earth's magnetic field. Experimentally the ability can be impaired by the presence of powerful magnets, so that we know this is not a fantasy. But we are still learning how the body achieves such remarkable navigational feats as have been objectively recorded time and again.

Dogs are also capable of predicting earthquakes and thunderstorms. When a thunderstorm is imminent they may become intensely alarmed, start panting and rushing about the house. They may even begin whimpering and trembling as if in some sort of pain. Their distress increases when the thunder starts to boom, but it can be observed some time before the storm actually breaks overhead. This sensitivity is a response to changes in barometric pressure and also possibly to alterations in the level of static electricity. It may seem meaningless behaviour today, but in the dog's wild ancestors it made good sense to become worried by these climatic signals. Wolves go to a great deal of trouble in selecting their burrows and dens. They build them on slopes where there will be a minimum of flooding, but even so a heavy downpour could prove fatal for tiny cubs. It is possible that domestic dogs rushing about the house when thunder threatens are behaving like wolf-cubs responding to the danger of flooding.

Some owners claim that their dog has, on rare occasions 'seen a ghost'. They are out for a walk with their pet on a summer's evening, crossing a field, when suddenly the dog halts and freezes. Standing rigid, it stares at nothing and its hair begins to rise on its shoulders and down its back. It starts to snarl and growl and perhaps even to whine, but it refuses to budge an inch when its owner attempts to move it. Then, as suddenly as the behaviour began, it ceases and the dog goes on its way. Anyone who has experienced such a moment finds it hard to forget the intensity of the dog's reaction, and it is easy to see why they insist that the animal 'saw a ghost'. The truth is that it probably detected a particularly strong scent deposit, not from another dog, but from some other animal species, such as a fox or a polecat. The strangeness of such a scent and the strength of it to the dog's sensitive nose are enough to account for the powerful response.

One of the most amazing claims for a dog's 'sixth sense' was made recently by research workers who reported that they had discovered infra-red detectors in the dog's nose. This could explain certain previously 'supernatural' abilities of some breeds. St Bernard dogs, for example, are said to be able to tell whether a climber buried in an avalanche is still alive or not, simply by sniffing into the snow. If there are sensitive heat-detectors in the noses of the animals, this theory is not so far-fetched. Furthermore, it has long been known that such heat-receptors do exist on the snouts of certain species of snakes, where they are used to detect the presence of small, warm-blooded prey. The fact that they exist at all in the animal kingdom strengthens the case for their existence in dogs.

XLIV

WHY IS A SAUSAGE-IN-A-ROLL CALLED A HOT-DOG?

THERE IS NO TRUTH IN THE RUMOUR THAT THE HOT-dog acquired its name because it once contained dog-meat, although long ago this idea did seriously damage their sales. The hot-dog was the brainchild of an American called Harry M. Stevens. It was his job to feed the huge crowds that attended the stadium where the New York Giants played their football games at the turn of the century. Hot frankfurter sausages had become a new food craze, but they were too messy to distribute around the grandstands of the stadium. Then he hit on the idea of encasing them in long, hot bread rolls and they were an immediate success, sold by vendors wandering around the aisles. They were at first called 'red-hots', because, as well as the freshly cooked sausage and the heated roll, Stevens had added a liberal smear of hot mustard. But then, in 1903, the famous sports cartoonist 'Tad' (T.A. Dorgan) made a drawing portraying the frankfurter inside the roll as a Dachshund. It was he who coined the name hot-dog, which quickly became popular. Unfortunately, it backfired when someone queried whether it meant that there really was some dog-meat involved in the production of the sausages, and sales rapidly slumped. The situation became so serious that the local Chamber of Commerce had to issue an official statement banning the term hot-dog from all advertisements. But you can't keep a good name down, and it eventually crept back into common usage. Today it is understood worldwide.

ACKNOWLEDGEMENTS

The publishers thank the following photographers and organisations for their kind permission
to reproduce photographs in this book:

1 Marc Henrie; 2 Tony Stone Images/Van Welsen; 3 Oxford Scientific Films/The Photo Library/Mark Amos; 6 Tony Stone Images/Renee Lynn; 8 Jacana/Frederic; 9 Tony Stone Images/Chip Henderson; 10 The Image Bank/Steve Gruban; 11 Marc Henrie; 12 Explorer/St Marc; 13 Marc Henrie; 14 Tony Stone Images/Chris Warbey; 15 Adriano Bacchella; 17 The Image Bank/Stephen Lynch; 18 Adriano Bacchella; 20 DIAF/Eric Planchard; 21 Jacana/Brabancon; 22 Jacana/Mero; 23 DIAF/Eric Planchard; 24 DIAF/Eric Planchard; 25 Tony Stone Images/Sue Streeter; 26 Tony Stone Images/Mark Petersen; 27 Adriano Bacchella; 28 DIAF/Eric Planchard; 29 DIAF/R Rozencwa; 31 Marc Henrie; 32 NHPA/Gerard Lacz; 33 Marc Henrie; 34 Bruce Coleman/Jane Burton; 37 Oxford Scientific Films/Okapia; 39 (above) DIAF/Pratt-Pries; 39 (below) Adriano Bacchella; Animals Animals/Jerry Cooke; 43 Jacana/Herbert Schwind; 44 (above) Oxford Scientific Films/Okapia; 44 (below) Bruce Coleman/Stephen J Krasemann; 48 Adriano Bacchella; 51 Adriano Bacchella; 53 DIAF/Eric Planchard; 54 Oxford Scientific Films/Photo Researchers Inc; 57-62 Adriano Bacchella; 63 Jacana/Sylvain Cordier; 64 DIAF/Eric Planchard; 65 (above) Animals Animals/Jerry Cooke; 65 (below) Animals Animals/Ralph A Reinhold; 68 Bruce Coleman/Fritz Prenzel; 70 Frank Lane Picture Agency/T Whittaker; 71 Adriano Bacchella; 72 NHPA/Daniel Heuclin; 75 (above) NHPA/E A Janes; 75 (below) Marc Henrie; 76 Jacana/Elizabeth Lemoine; 79 (above) Frank Lane Picture Agency/N Biet/Panda; 79 (below) Marc Henrie; 80 Ardea/J M Labat; 81 Tony Stone Images/Chris Warbey; 82 Jacana/Laurent Borgey-Loyer; 85 Bruce Coleman/John Cancalosi; 86 Jacana/Henry Gallais; 87 Marc Henrie; 89 Tony Stone Images; 90 (above) Oxford Scientific Films/Okapia; 90 (below) Oxford Scientific Films/Okapia; 91 Explorer/P Forger; 92 Bruce Coleman/Jane Burton; 94 Explorer/C Cuny; 96 Bruce Coleman/Jane Burton; 97-98 Adriano Bacchella; 100 Hewerdine – Anthony; 101 Adriano Bacchella; 102 Wegler – Anthony; 104 Adriano Bacchella; 105 Jacana/Axel; 107 Adriano Bacchella; 108 Oxford Scientific Films/Animals Animals/Zig Leszczynski; 109 The Image Bank/David de Lossy; 111 NHPA/Gerard Lacz; 115 (above) Bruce Coleman/Jane Burton; 115 (below) Bruce Coleman/Jane Burton; 116 Frank Lane Picture Agency/David Dalton; 118 The Image Bank/G & M David de Lossy; 119 Tony Stone Images/Sue Streeter; 121 Bruce Coleman/Hans Reinhard; 122 Wegler - Anthony; 124 Jacana/Denis Cauchoix; 126 Bruce Coleman/Nigel Blake; 128 Adriano Bacchella; 129 (above) Marc Henrie; 129 (below left) Marc Henrie; 129 (below right) Bruce Coleman/Hans Reinhard; 130 (above) DIAF/Eric Planchard; 130 (below) DIAF/Eric Planchard; 131 DIAF/Eric Planchard; 132 Bruce Coleman/Konrad Wothe; 133 NHPA/E A Janes; 134 Tony Stone Images; 137 (above) Ardea/John Daniels; 137 (below) Ardea/Jean-Michel Labat; 139 Explorer/D Clement 140 Bruce Coleman/Jane Burton; 143 Marc Henrie.

The line illustrations throughout are reproduced by courtesy of Dover Publications.

By the same author

The Biology of Art
The Mammals
Men and Snakes (co-author)
Men and Apes (co-author)
Men and Pandas (co-author)
Zootime
Primate Ethology (editor)
The Naked Ape
The Human Zoo
Patterns of Reproductive Behaviour
Intimate Behaviour

Manwatching
Gestures (co-author)
Animal Days
The Soccer Tribe
Inrock
The Book of Ages
The Art of Ancient Cyprus
Bodywatching
The Illustrated Naked Ape
Catwatching
The Secret Surrealist

Catlore
The Animals Roadshow
The Human Nestbuilders
Horsewatching
The Animal Contract
Animalwatching
Babywatching
Christmas watching
The World of Animals
The Human Animal
Bodytalk